JAMES HUTCHISON STIRLING

LECTURES
ON THE
PHILOSOPHY OF LAW

AF809024

Elibron Classics
www.elibron.com

Elibron Classics series.

© 2005 Adamant Media Corporation.

ISBN 1-4021-9935-X (paperback)
ISBN 1-4021-1424-9 (hardcover)

This Elibron Classics Replica Edition is an unabridged facsimile of the edition published in 1873 by Longmans, Green, and Co., London.

Elibron and Elibron Classics are trademarks of Adamant Media Corporation. All rights reserved.

This book is an accurate reproduction of the original. Any marks, names, colophons, imprints, logos or other symbols or identifiers that appear on or in this book, except for those of Adamant Media Corporation and BookSurge, LLC, are used only for historical reference and accuracy and are not meant to designate origin or imply any sponsorship by or license from any third party.

LECTURES

ON THE

PHILOSOPHY OF LAW.

TOGETHER WITH

WHEWELL AND HEGEL, AND HEGEL AND MR W. R. SMITH,

A VINDICATION

IN A PHYSICO-MATHEMATICAL REGARD.

BY

JAMES HUTCHISON STIRLING,

F.R.C.S., AND LLD., EDIN.

LONDON:
LONGMANS, GREEN, & CO.

1873.

PREFACE TO THE LECTURES.

THESE Lectures on the Philosophy of Law, published in *The Journal of Jurisprudence and Scottish Law Magazine* for the months of January, February, March, and April, 1872, were, in the first instance, delivered to the Juridical Society of Edinburgh, on the evenings of the 9th, 13th, 16th, and 20th November 1871 respectively.

The first lecture, let me say in especial, will be found an introduction pretty well to Philosophy in general at present, for philosophy in general at present is pretty well *German* Philosophy; and such introduction was a necessity of the subject; for any explanation in Hegel's regard involves one in Kant's also, and these two men's ideas are German Philosophy in its "outcome." For I still believe the former with elimination, *on the whole*, of Fichte and Schelling, to affiliate himself directly to the latter. Fichte's general conception,—self-development of the ego, and from the ego, certainly lies in Hegel, with infinite suggestion as concerns method and general details; and the *student* cannot dispense with a knowledge, at least of the *Wissenschaftslehre.* As for Schelling, again, whose philosophical production the intervention of Hegel breaks, as it were, into two very different deliverances, I cannot help regarding his study as even less important to an understanding of Hegel than the study of Fichte. Of what I call the *two deliverances*, the second, Schelling's *positive* or *religious* Philosophy, I am disposed to regard as but the product of arbitrary, happy-go-lucky, *Vorstellung*, and not of the necessity of the *Begriff;* which, therefore, however genial, will soon cease to be read,—the rather that it has no *historical* value, inasmuch as, despite the influence of Hegel which animates it, it contains no understanding, and is no continuation of philosophy as Hegel left it. Ruge's judgment, though too sweepingly negative, may, perhaps, be regarded as decisive here.

It is different with the *Naturphilosophie*, and the *Transcendental Idealism;* these, though they *may* be eliminated, are certainly historical in their influence, and if the *student*, in the case of Fichte, is expected to master the *Wissenschaftslehre*, and even the *Naturrecht* and the *Sittenlehre*, he will be equally expected, in the case of Schelling, to master the two works just named, especially the *Transcendental Idealism*, which will always rank as Schelling's best and most important work historically. The work on "Freewill" deserves special mention, were it only that it is specially referred to by Hegel. It is possible too, that Hegel's attention was directed to Böhme by Schelling, and, if so, this also must rank as one of Schelling's merits.

It is Hegel, then, who may be regarded as directly receiving the *historic pabulum* from the hands of Kant; and that *pabulum* must be recognised as having been masterfully controlled by Hegel, into a form all his own, and, in a certain way, perhaps the most important yet,—in a certain way, perhaps even the final one. No man till Hegel, ever explicitly saw the *notion*, and no man till Hegel, ever built a direct system on it. This is certainly the most important philosophical achievement that has fallen to the lot of any man, and Hegel must be pronounced not only in *form*, but in *matter*, as original a philosopher as ever lived, and that notwithstanding all his debts to Kant, or whoever else. For it would be quite possible to represent and demonstrate all philosophy to be but *a series of attempts to find the notion*, of which only that of Hegel at long and last succeeded. And it is very remarkable that Schelling, during the twenty-three years he survived Hegel, failed to see this, the work of Hegel, and to continue it as what was, historically, *an der Zeit*. The *notion*, that is, whether applicable or not to the *details* of nature, must now, I think, be allowed to be applicable to nature as a whole, and still more certainly applicable to the world of man. Man's *life* is in the crutch of the antithesis between universal and particular, for what lies in the hollow of that crutch is *thought* itself. Thought, in truth, is *nothing but* the very antithesis named. But, named as it may be, it is certainly to the *Spannung* between particular and universal, that man owes at once his conscience and his generalisation, or, what is the same thing, his religions, and philosophies, and arts, and sciences, and politics. These last (politics), indeed, may suggest that in *their* necessity—the necessity of aggregation, society—lies the *birth of the universal;* and, accordingly, those to whom such suggestion occurs, may desire to found all again, like the *Aufklärung*, and especially the *Revulsion*, on the mere *νόμος*, the mere agreement of mankind. (See Schwegler on the *Sophists.*) A little reflection, however, will reveal that even so the principle undergoes no discredit; for even so, it must have been *implicitly* present, else there never had been its development. Further than that, at the heart of things generally, a divine element of universality must be recognised to lie in interpretation of them, in constitution of them.

These Lectures will, among other things, give, it is hoped, intelligence to all this,—precisely the assistance, perhaps, or even the revelation that is wanted, otherwise I shall have to confess to some disappointment.

I may mention that a respected correspondent has referred me to the *Institutes*, III., xv. i., as the authority for Dr Heron's derivation of the word *stipulatio;* but, at the same time, puts little stress upon it,—though doubtful also of the connection with *stipula*. (See note to last Lecture.)

THE PHILOSOPHY OF LAW.

LECTURE I.

I. AN INTRODUCTION TO PHILOSOPHY IN GENERAL.

GENTLEMEN,—My first word must be one of apology. That an individual who is not a lawyer should address a distinguished society of lawyers, and on their own science, has that in it—in direct statement at least—to suggest only audacity and presumption. This I have felt from the first; and I have, all along, experienced a genuine reluctance to accept this place. Nevertheless, you yourselves have so willed it, and I have simply obeyed. I comfort myself with the thought, too, that it is not strictly into law that I am required to go, but rather into philosophy, though only so far as philosophy has legal bearings. I comfort myself, moreover, with this other circumstance—that, viewing the state of your information in this connexion, whether private or public, I shall not be expected by you to handle this subject *proprio Marte*, but by the aid of another or others. Indeed, I may say at once that the result of my examination of a goodly pile of books, supplied to me by your own courtesy, was to convince me that not only was Hegel's statement the most valuable in itself, but that all the others of any importance were so saturated with it as to be unintelligible without *its* intelligence. The production of this intelligence, besides, is one of the most important things that at the present moment requires to be effected, at the same time that it is one in which my own slight ability is as likely to be serviceable as in any other, perhaps. The philosophy of law, then, which I shall exhibit to you is that which has been presented in full detail by Hegel in the separate volume expressly published by himself, and named "Outlines of the Philosophy of Right, or Natural Right and Political Science in Ground Plan"—constituting, as I believe, the most valuable product of its author. Of the rest—Trendelenburg, Röder, Hildenbrand, Heron, Austin, and all the others—I hope to be able to say a word before concluding. Let me recommend to you *now* only Hildenbrand, a work most accurate, most elegant, yet most easy, though steeped withal in the light of Hegel—a work, too, that shames our English books on the subject into impotent beggary.

My situation, then, gentlemen, before you is a somewhat peculiar one; and when I refer to it now, and all it implies, together with certain other circumstances of time, number, &c., known to some of you, as bearing on the composition of these lectures themselves, I wish to be understood as suggesting a few considerations in appeal to your indulgence, and I have no doubt that, with your well-trained minds, they will very readily be taken—*ad avizandum.*

It is my duty now, then, so far as my ability permits, to make you acquainted with the Philosophy of Right in the compass and character in which it presents itself, in its own place, within the system of Hegel. But that, as these very words suggest, entails some consideration of the system itself in which it is imbedded, and of which it forms a part; for only through a sufficient conception of that, the whole, with which it is in connection, and from which it rises, can we ever hope to arrive at an adequate knowledge of this, the part. Besides, it is an affair of common knowledge as regards Hegel, that, in his expositions, no matter presents itself which is not the product of his peculiar dialectic, at the same time that that dialectic itself takes origin from a single principle. A preliminary word, then, will be necessary on the general system of Hegel, its dialectic, and principle. In short, I fear I shall be necessitated to disclose to you—the "Secret of Hegel." Now, do not for a moment fear, however, that I am going to inflict on you anything very detailed or very abstruse. Whatever I shall tell you shall be very short, and very plain, and, after all, perhaps, no such tax on your attention. The possibility of this, of course, may—and very excusably, perhaps—be doubted. For example, it is told of one of my best friends that, a gentleman finding him occupied with my work on Hegel, and inquiring what he thought of "the *Secret,*" he answered, "Why, I think the author has *kept* it!" I believe I saw from the papers, too, lately, that some gentleman, examined somewhere as to the state of philosophy at Oxford, and asked particularly as to whether the Hegelianism supposed to be there now prevalent was in any way due to the "Secret of Hegel," had boldly answered —"No; that book only makes the dark darker!" I fain hope there may be mercy for this gentleman; but, in view of the state of conscience he must yet come to, I really am tempted to believe that he will have a great fear in the end of going to—a very bad place!

But, joking apart, the "Secret" of Hegel is once for all open, and there need be no such very great difficulty in its regard—hard though Hegel may be to *read* after revelation of every secret. It appears to me that Mr. Lewes himself has at last found this to be the case. Not that I believe him yet truly to *judge* Hegel; but in the re-written article "Hegel," of the new edition of his "History of Philosophy" just published, he will be found to quote from my work on Hegel at least one passage in which it appears to me the *Secret* is very fairly *named.*

But, be all that as it may, I think I shall have no difficulty in finding, in characterization of the general procedure of Hegel, the short preliminary word we require here.

If it is possible to shut up Kant in a sentence, it is equally possible, in a sentence, to shut up Hegel. But Kant *has* been so shut up, and, as I believe, more than once. Here, from the "Note" on Kant in the second and third editions of the translation of Schwegler, is what I consider one such sentence: "The sensations of the various special senses, received into the universal *à priori* forms of space and time, are reduced into perceptive objects, connected together in a synthesis of experience, by the categories." Those who do not understand such phrases as "universal *à priori* forms," "perceptive objects," "synthesis of experience," "categories," &c., will probably know just as little of Kant *after* this sentence as they did *before* it. Nevertheless, that is no impeachment of the truth of the assertion that this sentence *does* contain all the broad outlines of the *cognitive* theory of Kant; and perhaps a word or two of explanation will demonstrate this—an explanation which I hope you will presently find to be in place. We can all fancy an ego, an I—fancy it as a unit or unity, as the primal unit, the primal unity. Well, to feel, to know, this unit must be, so to speak, *charged* with something, an *object.* Now this object, whatever it be, has parts, it possesses a certain breadth, it is, as compared with the unit into which it is received, a complex, a manifold; and it is by connecting the various units of this manifold to each other and to itself that the primal unit or unity, the ego or I, can come to possess, or, what is the same thing, to *know* an object. In an act of cognition, the primal unit, the I, then, reduces into its own unity the plurality of some manifold or object given to it. But the I does not effect this its function of unity, its uniting power, only in a single way. The I is strictly judgment, or the *I in act* is strictly judgment; and judgment, as we know from logic, has twelve subordinate forms or functions, which functions are arranged by threes under the more general functions of quantity, quality, relation, and modality. We see now, then, the general constitution of the subjective factor in an act of knowledge, of what concerns the I as I. As regards the other factor in the same act, the object again, it is always a *many* or manifold of special sense in space and time. Now, as for space and time, they are (to Kant) neither notions nor sensations; not the latter (sensations), for they are not due to any special sense, and they have not objects like other special sensations; and not the former (notions), for, viewed in the relation of wholes and parts, they are seen to have the constitution, not of something intellectually or logically understood, but of something sensuously perceived. Time and space, then, Kant reasons, being neither notions nor sensations, *and being at the same time universal and necessary,* must be pronounced general perceptive forms, *à priori,* or native to the mind, and lying in the mind from the first as necessary pre-conditions of special sense. This last—special sense—again, is, in all its forms, a mere affection of the subject exposed to the object. For, in all cases, an unknown object, or, as Kant calls it, a transcendental object, is to be supposed to act on special sense and excite the correspondent subjective affection. Here, now, then, we have a view of Kant's whole world; so far, at least, as cognition is concerned. There are the various affections of the various special senses (colours, feels, &c.); these are received into the general perceptive forms of space and time; and, finally, through the twelve different categorical modes of it, they are reduced into the unity of self-consciousness, or the ego. Should I repeat the sentence, and say now, then, "the sensations of the various special senses, received into the universal *à priori* forms of space and time, are reduced into perceptive objects, connected together in a synthesis of experience, by the categories," I think it will perhaps be less difficult for you to realize what is meant by Kant's *cognitive* theory being shut up in it.

As for Hegel, we must understand him to have started from these constructions of Kant, and only to have modified them. To him Kant's great want was that of *process,* process deductive, process interconnective. Starting with the I, the ego, he (Hegel) would have, like Fichte, the whole foison of the universe derived from its one primal and, so to speak, constitutive act. Accordingly it is not enough for Hegel to take up, like Kant, abstract logic as it presents itself and say, there are twelve classes of logical judgment, and these represent twelve functions of unity in self-consciousness, or the ego. Hegel must see the ego develop out of its own self, according to its own law, according to its own rhythm, according to its own principle, according to its own special, original, and primitive nature—develop into the entire system of its own constituent *inner* furniture or contents. And in this we see, too, how Hegel differs from Fichte. Fichte assumes a sort of *external* law of thesis, antithesis, and synthesis, according to which he *externally* develops the ego into its own constitutive variety. Hegel will have nothing to do with such *externality* of procedure; he must see the ego unfolding itself into its native variety, according to its own native principle, according to its own inner nature.

Well then, having accomplished this—and you are simply to consider it done—having developed the ego, by its own law, into its own inner contents, Hegel will not, like Kant, only conceive it endowed further with two subjective perceptive forms, two subjective cones of projection, and a variety of special sensational affections, which, received into and externalized by these cones, becomes reduced by the categories, or functional unities of the ego, into the innumerable special objects, and the one system, of experience. No; that is for him still external, and still arbitrary procedure; it is for him unwarranted procedure, which he must reject; and he conceives instead, after the internal process has reached its full sum, the same law to continue, and externalization of the whole internal sum to be the next result—externalization, that is, into this outward world of things. There is Nous to Hegel, thought, which in obedience to its own law, *in*volved into its own *inner* constituent sum, is further, in obedience to the same law, *e*volved into its own *outer* constituent sum, and that is the formed universe as it exists around us. In relation to Kant, then, it is to shut up Hegel in a single sentence to say he conceives the ego to develop into its own categories, and these being complete, externalization to result from the same common law. Still Hegel, unlike Kant, thinks not of the particular ego—yours and mine—in this process, but of the universal ego. So, to him, the ego completed in its own inner, is Nous, thought, universal self-consciousness—God, "as He is in His eternal essence before the creation of nature or any finite spirit." This is fairly the amount of the pretension of Hegel when he so describes his logic as such "exposition" (Darstellung) of God. But this being the case, then, God's universe to Hegel is plainly but the *contre-coup*—the counter-stroke of God's own inner nature. This universe is only to him in externality what God is in internality; or it is in externality only what *self-consciousness* is in internality.

These, then, are the leading ideas of these two men, Kant and Hegel, so far as *theory*, or *cognition*, is concerned; and if one sees in them great similarity, one sees in them also great difference. In Kant's world there is no knowledge of any *noumenal* existence. Although he postulates things in themselves—that is, independent outer objects, to set up the affections of sense in us: these affections (only farther manipulated from within) alone constitute for him all that can be called things. And though he postulates a *logical* unity for self-consciousness, he *knows* no *existential* unity to correspond to the word *soul:* what we call our affections from within, as well as what we call our affections from without, are only *phenomenally* known. In fact, all that Kant knows are phenomenal affections, phenomenally projected into optical spectra of externality, and then *logically* gathered in into unities again. Whether as regards the subject or as regards the object, he is quite destitute of any noumenal knowledge. *Without* is but sensation; *within* is but sensation; both are but stretched on two spectral skeletons, time and space, to be construed thence into what is called *experience.* The logical element is the only one in Kant that seems to possess any noumenal character, and that, too, rather in reference to *validity* than to *existence.* There is room in Kant, that is, for attaching to his logical element the character of noumenal or objective *validity,* but scarcely that of noumenal or objective *existence;* for self-consciousness being only logical in his eyes, his whole logical element is left without any substantial basis of support—unless in the mere postulate of an *inner* thing in itself, as there is a postulate of *outer* things in themselves. Now Hegel, though starting from these ideas, and deeply influenced by the importance of the logical element, still arrives in the end at a construction very different. The ego is not phenomenal to him, but noumenal; then the furniture of the ego is not limited to these twelve categories, but develops, and with rigorous necessity in every step, into a vast rich system. The spectral perceptive forms of space and time again do not exist for him in that character: they are the universals of externality, but externality to him is necessary, objective, and actual. These, then, are great improvements on the scheme of Kant, and there results a theory which, supplied with an actually external time and space, and an actually external world, is not repugnant to common sense. It is in his conception of externality and externalization, indeed, that we have one of the happiest characteristics of Hegel. "God said, Let there be light, and there was light:" the summed internality burst into its accurately correspondent externality: the flash of light was the birth of the universe. Directly we understand Hegel's dialectic, there is no difficulty at all in *conceiving* internalization as internalization *here*, and externalization as externalization *there*, but both together as mutually complementary co-factors, as correspondent pieces of one whole: they are the counterparts of the single tally. And in that case, also, it is not difficult to understand that all farther characters of externality will flow from the very idea of externality as externality. There will be consequently a boundless possibility of outness, a boundless side by side of particulars, all material, but boundlessly *different*. It is but in obedience to the general conception, too, that externality itself is not an absolute chaos; that the shadow of the tree of intellect falls on it, controlling it, and that it returns in circles, narrowing and narrowing, up to the thought, the internality from which it started, or from which it fell. In regard to this Hegelian theory of externalization, I recollect one of our most famous citizens to have exclaimed to me "I cannot take in all that d—d nonsense—do you mean to say that thought made granite?" But I really do not see this to be so very difficult: it lies in the fact that in externality as externality there must be boundless material *difference*: granite is simply one of the *differences*. Altogether, I must acknowledge myself to find Hegel's plan of externalization the happiest ever yet proposed—a plan necessary even when we say, as we *do* say, and *must* say, God *made* the world, for it answers the question of *how*—precisely that question how God, how thought, made granite, for example.[1]

[1] The moment the idea of externality *as* externality is seized, the great difficulty will be found at an end. One ought to ask one's self what *must* the *idea* of externality—what must *externality* itself be? Or, suppose you have *internality* completed—an ego, a boundless intussusception of thoughts, all in each other, and through or thorough each other, but all in the same geometrical point—what must *its* externalization—and its externalization is accurately externalization as externalization—be? *Its* externalization

From this account it will be evident, then, that Hegel is an idealist only as Aristotle is an idealist: he, like the Greek, would simply reduce all things to *notions*, would simply reduce all things to an ultimate generalization; and for what is ordinarily called *idealism*, he has not only no sympathy but an absolute contempt. Absolute or objective idealism is to him only *the thinking of the universe;* but *subjective idealism* is that spurious idealism which would make externality due to the internality of each *particular* subject, and then, for that simple act, take a big air as if it were philosophy. Hegel rejects such conception and such pretension utterly, and he is never tired of telling us so. In effect, it is a very insufficient reflection this, that because a knower can only know within, therefore there is no independent external universe; but that is really the *bulk* of what is called *subjective idealism*.

There is another side from which the work of Hegel may be regarded. It is that of *explanation in general*, explanation as such. Man may go on as much as he likes in his merely animal capacity, marrying, doing business, journeying here and there, and enjoying his senses in general: he finds always in the end that that is not enough; that he must *think* as well as live and enjoy; above all, that *he must think existence;* that he must inquire why, once for all, *all this is here*, *why* is it, *whence* is it, *whither* does it go? All that may be summed up in the single phrase: he demands *explanation*. Now, of course, there are a great many explanations now-a-days. Since Bacon, and, above all, Newton, there is what is called science. Explanation is sought for as regards the stars, and there is astronomy. Explanation is sought for as regards the atmosphere, and there is electricity say. Explanation is sought for as regards the constituents of the earth, their inter-relations, their inter-combinations, &c., and there are the sciences of physics, chemistry, and what not. Well, now, all these sciences are explanatory, science in general is an explanation; but these sciences, or science itself, are an explanation *within conditions* (the stars and planets themselves, the air itself) —within condition of the element itself, so to speak, which consti-

---

—it being an *in*ternalization—must plainly be the opposite of its ownself: whatever internalization *is*, externalization will be *not;* just as darkness and cold *are* precisely what light and heat are *not*. Or, taking it from the other end, we *see* that *externality* is infinite *out and outness*, infinite *difference*, under infinite *external* necessity (or, what is the same thing here, *contingency*); while *internality* again, is, and must be, infinite *in and inness*, infinite *identity*, under infinite *internal* necessity (or, what is the same thing here, *reason*). We can see here, too, the origin and meaning of Hegel's constant words, *negation*, and the *negative*. Externality is the negative of internality. But the former is the particular, while the latter is the universal: therefore the particular is always the negative of the universal. This may serve to show how deeply *logic* enters into *existence*. The same connection finds meaning for Hegel's perpetual *abstract*. Abstraction, in general, is to take any character in isolated self-identity; and that is the same thing as wresting any one *moment* apart from its connection with the rest into isolated self-identity—the work of *understanding*, not *reason*.

tutes their *nidus*. That element, that nidus, is simply taken as we find it, and, after every explanation of science in regard to the special laws of it, the questions in general, why, whence, whither? remain unanswered. These questions in general constitute philosophy. We shall not stop to consider that these "questions in general" constitute religion. We shall confine ourselves to philosophy. Philosophy, then, receives all the explanations of the sciences, of science in general, and, so instructed and prepared, proceeds to put the final question, the questions in general, why, whence, whither? In a word, philosophy demands an explanation of existence as existence. It is all very well to say here, *that* is impossible, that is a demand that, by the very conditions of the case, never can be granted. This is the situation pretty well of general belief at present: there is now a renunciation of metaphysics, there is now a renunciation of religion. This renunciation can never quash the essential need, however. Man is reason, and reason is irrepressible. Reason knows itself the essence of this universe, the essence of existence, and would see itself as it is, in its own grounds, in its own connections, in its own system. In a word, reason demands explanation as explanation. Now, what is that? What is explanation as explanation? And here it is that Hegel steps in. He considers the general nature of the case, and sees how its conditions *must* be. An explanation, to be an explanation, says Hegel, *must* be *so* and *so*. Now, in this he is not singular: all philosophers who *are* philosophers have seen the same thing. The philosophers *before* Socrates, Plato, Aristotle, Plotinus, Proclus, Descartes, Spinoza, Leibnitz *after* him, have all, more or less consciously, been led, in their philosophizings, by the same want. It would be easy to illustrate this in the case of all of them. I shall only, with this view, refer to Diogenes the Apolloniate. The object of this philosopher, as represented in the first two or three fragments of his writings collected by Mullach (they occur also in Ritter and Preller), is plainly explanation, explanation as a general problem. As necessary presuppositions to that end, he assumes that there must be *a single first* principle; that this principle must be *indisputable;* that it must be *adequate* to the *entire* existent *variety;* and that consequently it must possess intelligence—for intelligence in actual fact *is*. Some of his particular expressions, literally translated, are these: "All things that are must be but alterations of one and the same thing, and therefore the same thing; for if the things that are now—land, and water, and the rest—were different the one from the other, each in its own nature, and were not the same thing variously changed, it would be impossible that they could be mixed together or bring each other advantage or disadvantage: all things, then, are alterations of one and the same thing—at one time so and at another time thus, and they return to the same thing. But this thing must be great, and mighty, and eternal, and immortal, knowing much. For without intelligence it could not be so disposed as to possess *measures* of all things, of winter and summer, and night and day, and rains, and winds, and calms. And, in the same way, whoever considers them will find all other things disposed as beautifully as possible."

There is involved here, as is evident, a sort of *à priori* reasoning; as about the necessity to explanation of a common principle; how could things combine together or act on each other unless they participated in a common principle, that is pretty well the thought throughout. The further thought, too, is that, in view of the evident measure, proportion, rule, design according to which all things are disposed, this common principle can only be thought as intelligent: if there is rule, reflection, calculation in the effect, there must equally be rule, reflection, calculation in the cause. So it was, then, with Diogenes of Apollonia: *before* explaining, he determined the necessities *of* explaining; and so it was, also, with many of the others; so it was, above all, and in a supreme degree, with Hegel.

Hegel said to himself, or seems to have said to himself, for there is little that is direct in Hegel—he builds his system as a man might build a house, and lets us find out all his thoughts about it for ourselves—I, too, like other philosophers, would like to explain existence; but what does that mean? Evidently, I must find a single principle, a single fact *in* existence, that is adequate to all the phenomena *of* existence, to all the *variety* of existence; and this principle, while adequate to all the variety of existence, while competent to reduce into its own *identity* all the *difference* that is, must bring with it its own reason for its own self, its own necessity, its proof that it is, and it alone is, that which could not *not* be. This for explanation, ultimate, radical, and all embracing explanation, is evidently the necessary presupposition. It will plainly never do to *feign* a principle, to *fancy* a principle: the principle must *be*, an actual denizen, an actual thing present in *that which is*. The Red Indian who exclaims of all that he sees, of thunder and lightning, of the gas when it is lit in a theatre possibly, Manou! Manou! does not explain: he only exclaims; he only excites the imagination of his hearers into the vision of a monster, of a creature of fancy, of a mere Vorstellung, that is only assumed or said to have such and such power, to be such and such a cause. It does not explain rain to say there is a spout above the clouds, although there are minds which would find themselves quite contented with such a mere hypothetical image. Such mere hypothetical, *vicarious* image of phantasy, is not enough for Hegel then: he must find in that which actually is an all-fertile, an all-competent single principle. And here we see at once the reason of Hegel's dislike to the infidel god, the Gallic god, le dieu français—that *être suprème* of Enlightenment, of the Illumination, that is an empty abstraction, a barren image of phantasy on which all only *is to be* hung. But that is no prejudice to Hegel's prostration before God, before the true God, before that which is the eternal centre and root, and everlasting substance of the world.

He really and truly believes in God, but not in God that is only a topical god, a circumscribed, limited, particular something that is fancied up there, an enormous big man in the air that it is not absurd for Lalande the astronomer to try to see with his telescope. He has thought too much for that, he has read too much for that, he knows his catechism too well for that. He knows that God is a Spirit, that we cannot by physical searching find God out, but that we must worship Him in spirit and in truth. To that, at all events, his own words fairly amount.

This apart, then, Hegel, believing himself to acknowledge the true God, and averse only to the abstract god of the Aufklärung, would find an explanation of all that is in some *actual constituent* of all that is. And that is thought, reason; that is *self-consciousness*. Self-consciousness he finds to be the one aim of existence: all that is, *is*, he finds *only for self-consciousness*. That is the one purpose of existence. Nature itself is but a gradual and graduated rise up from the dust of the field to the self-consciousness of man. This we can see for ourselves: in the inorganic scale, up and up to the organic, and, in this latter, up and up to man. All is *explained* only when it is converted into thought, only when it is converted into ourselves, only when it is converted into self-consciousness. But if all only *is* for self-consciousness,—if all can be converted into self-consciousness—if self-consciousness is the substance and the ultimate of all, then self-consciousness can be regarded as that which *instituted* all, self-consciousness can be regarded as the *prius* of all: all is only there for it, and to be explained into it. In this way, it is seen, then, that self-consciousness is the principle of all —in other words, that self-consciousness is the principle of explanation sought. Hegel's work, consequently, is but one of ultimate *generalization*, of ultimate *induction*. *Of actual facts*, he finds self-consciousness the dominant one, the key to, and the *raison d'être* of all the rest. What follows, then, is that Hegel should apply this key.

Of course, there are many men now-a-days, as I may just stop to remark, who only scorn as futile any such attempt as this of Hegel, and to the sentiments of these men we find from Xenophon that Socrates long ago gave voice and authority "For *he* did not, like most of the others, debate of the nature of this all, speculating as to how what the Sophists call the world came into being, and by what necessities the various heavenly bodies were produced . . . and he wondered if it was not evident to these men that it was impossible for man to find out these things." These words occur in the very first chapter of the *Memorabilia*, and there are more beside them to the same effect, with general derision of these high speculative philosophers, who yet, as is further pointed out, with all their claims, have hardly an opinion in common. This the opinion of Socrates is a very decided one, then. Hegel knows it well, too, but he does not let it trouble him. Rather, in direct opposition to

Socrates, and to Socrates as praised by Cicero, he boldly exclaims "philosophy cannot be worth anything to the lives and homes of men, unless it come down from heaven; and it is the one duty left us to carry it up into heaven." In this, it is certain that, apart from that of Socrates, the highest names can be placed on the side of Hegel. Indeed it is difficult to find a single name on the whole bright file which did not belong to one whose reflection was such as fell within the censure of Socrates. Plato and Aristotle directly followed him; but the favourite speculation of both lay, we may say, *in the heavens*, and this not less in the case of the real Aristotle than in that of the ideal Plato. These names shall suffice, then, for the side of Hegel, and we shall let all the others, modern or ancient, pass. In a word, as I said already, *reason* demands an explanation of existence as existence; and *we must* obey *reason.*

On the part of Hegel, we shall see now, then, his application of the key of self-consciousness for this purpose. It was by induction, as we saw, that Hegel came to this key. Self-consciousness is in the world of facts, and all these other facts are only for it. *It* is the ultimate and essential drop of the universe, and explanation is only the reduction of all things into it. All things, indeed, stretch hands to it, rise in successive circles ever nearer and nearer to it. Now what is self-consciousness? Its constitutive movement is the idealization of a particular through a universal into a singular, or, taking it from the other end, it is the realization of a universal through a particular into a singular. Now that may appear a very hard saying, but it is a very simple one in reality: it is only a general naming of the general act of self-consciousness. In every act of self-consciousness, that is, there is an object and a subject. The object on its side is a material externality of parts, while the subject on the other side again is an intellectual unity, but a unity that has within it, or behind it, a whole world of thoughts. It is by these thoughts the subject would master the object, reduce it into itself. These thoughts, then, that thus master the object, are the universals under which it is subsumed, and it, as so subsumed, is but the particular to these universals. The outward world, then, consists only of the particulars of the universals that constitute the inward world. I think this will be readily seen to be true. We can only think by generalizing, and generalizing is the reduction of particulars to universals. Evidently, then, in every act of self-consciousness, particulars meet universals in a singular. We were right, consequently, in describing the constitutive movement of self-consciousness to be the idealization of a particular (the object) through a universal (the thought) into a singular (the subject). When we consider, moreover, that self-consciousness is the original substantial principle, the veritable *prius* of all, we shall see also that it is not incorrect to describe the constitutive movement of self-consciousness as the *realization* of a universal through a particular into a singular. Now, that is the Notion—that is the

Secret of Hegel. *The vital act of self-consciousness is the notion.* The single word *notio* involves all the three elements, a *knowing* (universal) of *something* (particular) in a *knower* (singular). An act of knowing—idealization quite generally—is the reduction of a particular through a universal into a singular; but *è contra, creation*—and that is realization quite generally—is the exemplification of a universal to a singular through a particular. This, then, is the one ground-notion which Hegel, by virtue of its own law, its own rhythm, as triple in its own form, and so triple that its units, though *different* from, are yet related to, and *identical* with each other—this, I say, is the one ground-notion which Hegel sees develop before him out of its own self into the sum of its own *inner* constituent system of notions. That inner system he then calls *idea.* The notion is the first and the ever present substance—every one of the derivative notions is but *the* notion—but the completed internal system of these notions, or of *the* notion, is *the idea.* The idea now, then, is the entire and complete universal, and it is only in obedience to the one ever-present law that it sunders into the particular—Nature. Nature again, the particular, returns to the universal in the singular, Mind, which gradually rises from its primal involution in nature up through all its forms to the Absolute Spirit.

Universal, particular, and singular are the three moments of the notion, and everything *organic,* everything *true* in this world is—however abstract its *element*—a *concrete* of these three moments, which can be seen to take on in the course of the development a thousand names, as thesis, antithesis, synthesis, or a form which is a great favourite in my own explanations, simple apprehension, judgment, and reason. This *notion* may be illustrated in a variety of ways. What is *organization,* for example—what is an organization to any purpose? Reflect on it as you may, you will find that it is the reduction of a *many* of particulars to the *unity* of a singular through the menstruum of universals—the plan and what it implies. Every concrete is but such organization. The family, for example: there is no perfect family where there is not the *fulfilled* IDEA, where each of the three moments, universal, particular, and singular, has not full justice accorded it. So the state; a state must be *idea*—perfect harmony of universal, particular, and singular, else it is imperfect and not a state. The state is the accomplished *idea* of the self-developing *notion*—here free-will, and in it, if perfect, each of the *moments* has its due place and its due scope. But is not the universe itself the best illustration? The universe itself is but the realization of the universal through the particular in the singular; and all that is said when we pronounce the single word—self-consciousness.

Hegel's work now, then, can evidently be called simply the ultimate *generalization.* He sees that if we would ultimately explain, we must fairly generalize explanation itself. Explanation is always the reduction of an object into self-consciousness; ultimate explanation, then, must be a reduction of all into self-consciousness. But self-consciousness is a fact, it is something *in rerum natura*, a principle actually existing: Hegel's work, then, is in so many words the final and universal *induction*.

But you will say, perhaps, the self-consciousness that is in nature is *ours*—there is no other self-consciousness *in nature* than ours: are we to suppose that Hegel views *my* self-consciousness, *your* self-consciousness, *his* self-consciousness as God? In one way, I cannot deny this. Still Hegel's idealism, as I said already, is no *subjective* idealism: he does not conceive nature to be an externalization of the *individual subjects'* categories, notions, but of those of the universal subject, of those of the universal self-consciousness. But Hegel, we might object further, would certainly admit that every individual finite subject might die, and yet the universe would subsist. What in that case were God? Would not Hegel seem simply to conceive then a potential God—a God as it were asleep in nature—and who had yet to be *realized* afresh in other finite self-consciousnesses? There are professing adherents of Hegel—Ruge and the so-called party of German critics—who seem to entertain some such conception. I, for my part, admit that such may appear to be the case, so far as Hegel's developments apart from time, apart from history, are concerned; but I assert such an appearance no longer to obtain the moment the development has entered the domain of spirit. In the sphere of religion, especially, Hegel, as is well known, sums up his development in Christianity as the revealed religion, and in the midst of numerous expressions that are unmistakeably theistic. I may quote here what I said in the newspapers (*Courant*, Dec. 21, 1868) on this head three years ago:—"We are bound to accept Hegel's own professions. Again and again, and in the most emphatic manner, he has asserted himself, not only to be politically conservative, but religiously orthodox—a Lutheran Christian. If we accept, as we do, his first assertion without difficulty, we have no right to deny his second. Indeed, however pantheistic the construction, so to speak, in space may appear, the tables, as intimated, are wholly turned in the construction in time, and Hegel ends not only by profession, but by philosophy, a theist and a Christian."

I may say also, that this statement met at the time with the complete approbation of the non-Hegelian Professor Ueberweg—non-Hegelian, but, before his death, as both correspondence and actual published writings led me to believe, less and less so. Ueberweg, whose premature death—the premature death of perhaps the most indefatigable philosophical student of his time—we are now justly lamenting, wrote me that his belief was quite mine as expressed in the quotation I have read, and that it was impossible to establish a negative against such a religious claim for Hegel. Of course, it is to be allowed that Hegel *philosophizes* Christianity, and that his understanding of much is not such as John Knox would have accepted. Nevertheless, this is to be said, that Hegel would have claimed accord—*substantially*—even with John Knox. We believe the same historical fact and facts, he would have said; only you see them in the *Vorstellung*, while I see them in the *Begriff*. That at all events is really the true nature of the case; and it is a piece of wisdom that is much needed at present. That single distinction between Vorstellung and Begriff is fitted to bring about perfect reconciliation between the beliefs of the less educated and those of the more educated, and give the Church peace. I may add, too, that every objection from the religious side that may be taken to the *rôle* assigned by Hegel to self-consciousness will disappear on due consideration of the text: "In His own image God created man."

Returning again for a moment to the principle of self-consciousness itself, let me point out another advantage possessed by it as a principle of explanation. It contains within itself both *difference* and *identity*, and a little reflection will make it plain that there can be no possible explanation of this world without a principle that contains both elements. The origin of *difference* in *identity* is the point and focus of the whole problem; but we have that at once in self-consciousness. Thought, reason, self-consciousness, is the one single necessity, the primal ἀνάγκη, that that could not *not* be, and alone that that could not *not* be; but thought, reason, self-consciousness, is by nature a duplicity in unity, difference in identity, for to know is to be always two things in one; what knows and what is known are for ever different but for ever identical. And so it is that evolution is possible; for, after all, the work of Hegel is certainly an *evolution*. It must be regarded, however, as only a *potential* one, only one *in idea*, not one that takes place or ever took place *in time*. And this gives it a vast superiority over ordinary evolution doctrines. To suppose that there ever was a natural first germ that *naturally grew* into another, as, for example, that the oyster ever *grew* into a man, is to suppose an absurdity. The evolution *is—there—in idea*—and that is really by power of the idea—but it never took place in *natural* fact. All that ingenuity which would explain the peacock's tail by the loves of the female (whose comparative plainness then remains unaccountable) is but perverse and a waste of time—a waste of time in this, too, that science is quite unable to allow the explanation itself *time enough*. It would be easy to bring forward sufficient ingenuity to explain the spider's web—by a drop of accidental fluid accidentally emitted by some certain spider one fine day, that gave that accidental advantage which is necessary; but would such ingenuity, such Vorstellung, such mere fancy, be scientific explanation? The method of *natural conjecture* in fact, however amusing, leads nowhere.

But let us now, in conclusion, just glance at Hegel's evolution that precedes and results in the notion of law, to which all that I have yet said is only preliminary; and I trust I have your excuse for spending so much time on what *is* only preliminary, my conviction being that any shorter previous explanation would have been futile. Hegel's system, as is now pretty well known, is contained in three great spheres—the Science of Logic, the Philosophy of Nature, and the Philosophy of Spirit. Here we see at once that what we have before us is the Notion. Logic is the universal; Nature is the particular; and Spirit is the singular. Logic, having developed into full *Idea*, passes into the particular as the particular, into externalization as externalization, in Nature; and Nature, rising and collecting itself, through sphere after sphere, from externality itself in the form of space, up to *natural* internality in the form of organic life, passes into Soul, which is the first form of Spirit. The instrument of the evolution all along, we are to understand, is the *Notion* in its three *Moments*. Omitting any closer consideration of the evolution in Logic and Nature—vast wholes of philosophy though they be—we shall pass to that of Spirit; and here, too, we must be but perfunctory only until we reach our own subject. The three heads under which Spirit is treated are Subjective Spirit, Objective Spirit, and Absolute Spirit—obviously again in agreement with the three moments of the Notion. Under Subjective Spirit we have mind rising *through its own faculties* to its own higher forms—or *the faculties themselves* are represented *but as successive stages* of development in mind itself—and all as ever in obedience to the *notion*. Thus, theoretical spirit, or the spirit that knows, cognition that is, being complete, passes into practical spirit, the spirit that acts, the spirit that has will; and will can only realize itself in the objective world of Law—in the State. And here we have reached at last our own subject. The introduction has been long, but not longer, I believe, than was absolutely necessary to enable us to understand the movement of Hegel—that dialectic which we shall find as active in what concerns Right, Law, as elsewhere. Now, however, I think we may consider ourselves fully *instruits*; and at our next meeting we shall effect the transition from the theoretical to the practical spirit, and enter on the objective domain of the latter—on the domain of will, and of law as its realization.

LECTURE II.

GENTLEMEN,—At our last meeting we saw the *Notion* of Hegel, and in its connection with Kant; for I still believe Hegel to affiliate himself in the main *directly* to Kant. Let him owe what he may, principally by way of suggestion, whether to Fichte or Schelling, it is really Kant's substance that Hegel carries further. We saw that an excellent clue to that Notion was explanation as explanation. Explanation, namely, as explanation, is a reduction to self-consciousness, and it follows that we have reached *the* ultimate when we have reduced self-consciousness to *its* ultimate. Now, that *is* the Notion. Or *the* notion is an act of self-consciousness *as such*—the perfect *generalization* of such act. This, then, is the creative germ of all and everything; and, as such, evidently it can be no blank self-identity: it must possess, in its own self, difference; and it must return from this its difference into that its identity again. No act of self-consciousness whatever but is seen to exemplify this abstract description. Self-consciousness so constituted, then, is conceived to develop itself, in obedience to its own inner law, first into its own *inner* system. This, the realization of the logical *notion*, is, and in connection with that notion, the logical *idea*. The idea now, as completed *inner* system, sunders, in Nature, into the *externalization* of its own self and of all its constituents—into a chaos, then, of infinite *physical difference* and infinite *physical contingency*. This chaos, however, re-collects itself, and returns in Spirit (Mind) to the Universal again. Mind now, or Spirit, appears in a succession of faculties, and rises through its subjective and objective forms into its absolute form—into Absolute Spirit. Subjectively, more particularly, it reaches, through stages of Perception, Conception, Thought, the full fruition of theoretical intelligence, and it is at the transition of this into Practical Spirit, into Will, that we have now arrived.

This transition it will not be difficult to understand, if we shall but fairly realize to ourselves what the completion of *theory* is. Theory when complete, that is, has converted its objects into itself. The objects of theory are indeed outer, but when it *understands* them it has fairly made them inner: all that they truly are, all that they substantially are, is now within. It has abolished their alienation, their foreignness, it has made them *its*—it has determined them *its*—it has *determined* objects as *its*. But intelligence that *determines* objects is Will. This is Hegel's transition from what we know in common parlance as the *intellectual powers* to what we know in the same parlance as the *active powers*, or this is Hegel's transition from theory to practice, from what he calls theoretical spirit or intelligence to practical spirit or will. We see at once that it is ingenious—that it is ingeniously figurative. Theory surveys an object, and *enjoys* its survey; but the *result* of such survey is to make the outward inward; and, if the outward is inward, it is theory's own, it is *determined* by theory, which is now will, and its *enjoyment* has become an *act*. Hegel, of course, does not expect us to see in this transition an actual fact in time, but only the *potential* connection of intelligence and will, only their connection *sub specie æternitatis*. And viewed so, it is perfectly credible; for intelligence and will are not in reality different, but the same: they are but action and counter-action of the same common life. Where the one is, the other is: will is but thought in act, thought is but will *in potentia*. It is, therefore, true in an absolute, or perfectly general, reference, that thought *of itself* determines itself into will, remaining, at the same time, the *substance* of it—of will. This, I think, will be seen to be true from the very nature of the case, and apart from the ingenious figurativeness of Hegel's steps, which are again briefly these:—To think an object is to understand it. The thinking of an object, then, is the birth of a new object out of or in the old object. But this new object belongs to thought; and this new object is at the same time all that is true in the old object. This new object is all that the old object really is—this new object is, in fact, the old object. But thought has thus manifested itself to determine an object, and thought that determines an object is will.

Will, then, is thought determining itself out of its own self into objects, or, as we more generally figure it, into action on objects—a difference of phrase, however, that makes no difference in the facts; for as we have just seen, our *action* on objects is to determine these objects as our own. They are indeed outer to us, but in that we understand them, we enter into them, we participate in them, we establish a community between them and us—that is, we make them ours.

But though there be this intimate connection between them, it is certain that will does not, in the first instance, *appear* as thought—appear, that is, on the stage of existence. Will, as we first *find* it, is, like everything else, *in a state of nature*. Will, as we so find it, even in man, is rather an instinct than a rational thought. The needs and greeds of the mere animal are the matter in which it first asserts itself. Nevertheless, man is essentially reason, and even in yielding to these needs and greeds, it is reason that comes gradually to the front. For example, will cannot yield even to these needs and greeds without *reflection*, and reflection, once begun, can only end in full-fledged reason. The needs and greeds are compared with their objects and the means of obtaining these. They are compared with each other. They are compared, however vaguely at first, with the chief end of man, thought, reason, which in all cases, is always at least *implicitly* present. The result of this comparison on the part of reflection is a subordination and classification of the various needs and greeds, of the various desires,—a subordination and classification that can only end in System. This system now is what we call happiness, and the needs and greeds, accordingly as they variously contribute in quality and quantity to happiness, are variously arranged and valued. But, after all, this arrangement never becomes perfect, never becomes satisfactory. The needs and greeds are even infinite; subject differs from subject in regard to them; according to times and seasons, subject differs from his own self in regard to them; the whole quest of what is called happiness manifests itself to be indefinite, obscure, and contingent; and let it end in what criterion it may, this criterion remains always an *enjoyment*, something subjective and contingent, something limited. In this way, then, it becomes plain that will can never content itself with what is called happiness as a final aim, and that there must be found for it an object wider, deeper, and more essential. This object can only be its own self. The only satisfactory final object to will can only be will. This is one of those expressions that is peculiarly perplexing and distressing to the English reader of the philosophical Germans. The difficulty, however, is only in the phrase and not in its import. As we have already seen, will is identical with thought, with reason, and when we substitute these synonyms in the phrase that will can only will will, all ambiguity vanishes. That the object of will should be will—this may appear an empty phrase, but it is not so when we say the object of *reason* is reason. Reason, we know, has realized itself in the world around us, in God's world; and it does not seem strange, with that fact before us, to say reason seeks reason. But reason has also realized itself in the world of man, in its body of laws, in its code of morals, in the general arrangements of what is called the State. Now when we know that it is will which has realized reason in law, morals, and state, it will no longer appear absurd to say will realizes its own self; the object of will is will, or will wills will. It will at once suggest itself to us, then, that the will so spoken of is thinking will, and thinking will is free will.

Of course, as we are all now educated in Great Britain, this is considered by all of us, or all but all of us, an absurdity; the supposition of free-will is an absurdity. Most modern English authorities are of this opinion, and they really have brought their public to the *same* opinion. Now, this state of opinion on the part whether of author or reader, results from *making judicious play* with what are called *motives.* We never act, it is said, but from a *motive;* this motive presents itself to us by *necessity of the case,* and it involves us in a like necessity. Some few writers seem to doubt this, and not to be sure that they cannot act without motives. Mr. Alexander, not long since, fairly posed Mr. Mill by asking him, having touched the left side of your nose, do you not *feel* that you *could* have touched the right instead? Notwithstanding the fairness of the question, and the earnestness of the "yes or no" with which it was followed up, Mr. Alexander, it appears, so far as I have learned, did not succeed in coaxing an answer from Mr. Mill. But, of course, we all *feel* that it is quite free to the great bulk of us at present to touch either side of our nasal prominence we please. Not that it will be altogether possible for us to exclude, *even in such a case as this,* what may be called the play of motives. Whether we elect to touch the right side or to touch the left side, it will be difficult to banish from our mind's eye what might be called a motive,—and a motive not a bit too trivial when compared with the action. We do not generally act without a motive, and, in fact, we feel ourselves in no circumstances at a greater loss than when that is required of us. Your socks lie there for you to put on of a morning, and it is really, for the most part, quite indifferent to you which shall be made right and which left. There is no doubt you *can* put *either* on the right foot, and you are really quite willing to *put* either on it; but you feel it a bore that such a question should have at all turned up. You sit there with your feet naked, feeling that but for the question they would have been clothed, and, motive or no motive, without difficulty. You are glad to compound for a motive by making right the sock nearest to the right foot, by closing your eyes and taking the first you catch, or even by tossing up to settle first choice. All this shows, however, how habitually man acts by motives, how impossible it is for him to act without motives, even in circumstances the most trivial and indifferent. Rather than act without a motive, we *shut our eyes, or we toss up.*

Now the true light on the matter is just a reversal of what is usually believed in England on this question. To act *by* motive is to act *freely,* to act without motive is to act *under necessity.* Possibly some of you may object here—We know that distinction already, but we remain unconvinced, for though *moral* necessity is not *physical* necessity, it is still *a* necessity, and compels obedience. But my answer is briefly, Physical necessity (and I beg you to observe that physical means *natural*—what is of mere *nature*)—physical necessity is the only necessity, and moral necessity is freedom. That only is free which is amenable solely to its own self; but in obeying moral motive it is my own self—my own inmost, deepest, truest self I obey; and, therefore, it is that in the very obeying of it I am free, and all the more free the more thoroughly moral it is—the more thoroughly it is my own self. In the case of the socks no motive was present, and I was not free; to free myself I had to shut my eyes, I had to toss up, or I had arbitrarily to invent a motive and take the sock nearest. Now, what I call being bound in regard to the socks, is what would be generally stated in England as a proof of freedom; whereas, what would appear very generally a proof of necessity in England would possibly, according to the views which I adopt, be used as a proof of freedom. Thus, as regards the socks, I should be held free in England so long as I was *without* motive, and bound only when in *obedience to a motive*, I put the *one* rather than the *other* on the right foot. Now my way is to reverse this. Should I discover, for example, that the one sock had been worn on the right foot the day before, and decide, for economical motives, to give it the benefit of a change and wear it on the left foot to-day, I should really be acting in freedom, for I should be acting according to reason,—I should have *a reason* for my action, I should have *a motive* for my action.

Really Kant and Hegel have completely determined this question. Kant is nowhere more convincing than precisely here, and it is precisely here that he is ever eloquent. What fine pictures he gives us in this cónnexion of how a man acquires the esteem of others, acquires his own esteem, just in proportion to the completeness with which he tramples on *commodity*, on self-interest, and yields to the universal—to moral motive—and that without hope, without chance of reward! Accordingly, it is quite clear to Kant that, besides *empirical* motives—that is *sensuous* motives, or, as he otherwise calls them, *material* motives, *pathological* motives—there are motives of *ideas*, motives from *within* and not from without, *actual prescripts of reason unto its own self*. If motives were only empirical, he argues, action would be only *hypothetically conditioned*, that is, the action would be viewed only as a means to an end. Reason in such circumstances could only assist in the discovery of the *advisable:* it could not command the *obligatory*. There would result only *prudential rules*, not laws of duty—directions, prescripts *technical* merely, suggestive of an *art* to be *ac*quired rather than a course of *conduct* to be categorically *re*quired. Where motive is empirical, will can only receive a *maxim*, not an *imperative command*; for an *empirical* object must act on *appetition*, on desire, must presuppose a craving subject under the influence of pathological feelings—inclination or aversion, &c. Maxims, then, are only subjective; and the most general expression for a subjective maxim is *self-love*, the general object of which again is felicity, happiness, one's own satisfaction. But felicity, as already said, though naming a *whole* of satisfaction, and though, in such generality, an ascension over the random contingency of particular desire, cannot furnish a *law;* it is but a general title over infinite diversity: no two, as we saw, are agreed on happiness: but even were there agreement among us as to the object of happiness, the foundation would still be pathological and contingent, devoid of the necessity of a law.

In fact, it is plain that Kant sees happiness, though a general name, to be still—as its aim is *enjoyment*—a *particular* desire. There *is*, then, a will that takes no note of happiness, that respects itself, and is respected just as it tramples down happiness, just as it tramples down self-love. This will, independent of all sensuous motive, obedient only to its own self in its own reason, to its own law, to its own categorical imperative, is free will. And how such pure rational *form*, free from all sensuous *matter*, should be adequate to objective commands, *à priori* binding, and universally necessary—to categorical injunctions good for all rational beings, it is not difficult to understand. Were it not so—were there not a practical voice of reason, unmistakeable, irresistible, clear, intelligible even to the commonest, it is plain to Kant that morality would be destroyed. I may mention here one or two of Kant's illustrations in his general support—"Labour when young not to starve when old:" here plainly there is a *condition* offered you, and the prescript is only *hypothetical*. This is not so, however, in the case of such a proposition as "you must not promise falsely:" there the command is categorical and direct. Kant asks, too, "under penalty of death, would you, at command of the King, give false witness for the destruction of an innocent man?" and points out that your own state of mind will prove that you *can* die rather than so act, as it is clear there that you at all events *ought* to. In this way, Kant shows the eye of duty to be bent forward to work only, and never thrown backward to consequences. That active duty is attended by a sense of doing what is right, which may be called satisfaction, cannot be doubted; but it is not for this satisfaction—it is not for the satisfaction expected—it is only for the command given that duty acts. Many a one has died for duty, at the stake or on the wheel, with scarcely a feeling but that of the physical suffering, knowing only that it was *necessary* for him so to do. It is absurd, then, to convert *moral satisfaction* into *pleasure* (eudæmonism), and assert the same to be the sole rule of action. That man must have a disinterested nature—that man must be thankful for small mercies, who can see in such cases (as death on the wheel or at the stake) a *satisfaction* for the *enjoyment* of which he would readily die! It is thus, then, that Kant, contrasting subjective, empirical, contingent, hypothetical maxims, dependent on pathological, material desire, with objective, pure, apodictic, categorical imperatives, dependent on absolute form of reason—it is thus, I say, that Kant in the existence of the latter makes good the fact of free-will.

In this matter Hegel only follows Kant, bringing ultimate abstraction to all, ultimate completion, ultimate system, ultimate support. He, too, accentuates free-will—that to Hegel also is the whole ground and basis of the practical world. "The object of the science of Right," he tells us, "is the human will, with special reference to the relation of the *particular* to the *universal* will;" and free-will, accordingly, is that will which hears the universal only—

which implicitly obeys the universal—let the interest of the particular be what it may. He contrasts the phenomena of will with those of physical nature, and insists on the inapplicability of the law of causality to the former. In this law he observes the cause, but *repeats* itself in the effect—the motion in the ball is the same motion that was in the bat, the water on the street is the same water that was in the rain-cloud—but we see no such identity between the *motive* and the *act* of will. The *motive* does not repeat itself in the *act:* the act is the expression not of the *nature of the motive,* but of the *nature of the agent* who is simply roused to put *himself* into operation. Here it is no mere effect that we see passively repeating the necessity that lay in the cause, but a wholly new power in act, a power that meets actively what comes to it as motive, that changes its direction, that modifies it, and can even *negate* it. "Circumstances and motives," exclaims Hegel, "master a man only so far as *he yields to* them. . . . He who appeals *for excuse* to such influences only degrades himself into a thing of *nature:* his act is his own, not that of somebody else, not the effect of something external to him." But Hegel goes systematically to work here, and displays at large the nature of the will, and according to every movement of the notion. The will, in fact, is an excellent illustration of the notion, for the will is concrete, the will just *is* the notion. The will is the Begriff, that that ideally begrips or be-grasps all, that that ideally involves or implies all; or it is that in whose pure negativity, in whose pure self to self ideality, the whole foison of the universe potentially lies. *So,* it is specially in its own form proper; *so,* it is specially *universal.* Will can retire into its own self, will can abstract from all and everything, will is the possibility of pure universality. It is this possibility that is the condition of volition itself: without this power of reflection, without this power of abstraction, it would be in vain to talk of volition at all, which only *is,* if it *can* keep itself indefinite. This then is the moment of universality in will in which it abstracts from every determinate state of its own self, and, under every determination, remains indeterminate and equal to itself. Man can abstract, in suicide, from his very life: the beast cannot, whatever anecdotes to the contrary may be told to amuse us.

But the will cannot remain abstract, it must *realize* itself; *universal* will must pass into *particular* will, and the question now is, *What* shall be willed? If only the gratification of our sensuous needs and greeds, then evidently what is willed is something foreign to will itself, something limited, something contingent. Will, even there, knows itself not the particular greed, and capable of denying such. This is freedom, but it is only freedom *in form,* only *formal* freedom; it is not *material* freedom, not freedom *in matter:* and without freedom in matter, there can be no true freedom, no free-will. To that it is necessary that will should will its own self. And this is the *singular,* this is the moment of singularity: here will is present only with its own self, and so free. But how shall will will its own self? How otherwise than by willing its own thought. Will is but thought, thought is but will. Free-agency is the realization of one's own self, but that is thought, and the realization of thought as thought can only take place in ethical institutions—in Law, Morality, and the State.

In exposition and illustration of these three moments of will much can be alleged, and, by Hegel, has been alleged. A word or two in regard to this must now suffice however—

As regards universality, for example, that is really just one aspect of man as capable of generalization, as the power that generalizes. The focus, the *punctum vitale* in man, is simply generalization, which is only another word for thought. But to generalize thought is the same thing as to universalize will. The *beast* is driven ever by an *individual* conception, by an *individual* motive; but man in both respects will be controlled—ultimately—only by the *universal*. And what a difference this makes one can see without difficulty. To *have* a habit—as a beast may have—is one thing, but to *know* I have a habit is quite another thing. In this latter case reflection has set in; the habit is not only known, but what is other to it, its opposite is known, and a judgment that may negate the habit becomes at once possible. The particular, in short, is now received into the universal, and may disappear there. There are times when such disappearance becomes the one historical fact. During the French Revolution, it was the *universal* of will alone functioned. Every *particular*, accordingly, was nought—even the particulars, particular after particular, then and there suggested—and madness ruled the hour, destruction was the lord of all. Not a single particular, not one *difference* could be tolerated, whether rank, or birth, or fortune, or talent, or virtue, or even beauty. That will can withdraw itself into the abstract universal, and become *actively* the universal void, is here evident, just as it is evident that it can become also, in the worship of Brahma for example, the *passive* void.

As concerns will in *particularity* again, that form is familiar to all of us, for it is will, as each of us, for the most part, uses it. This is the form that is commonly either opposed or defended as free-will, and, as we have seen, both opposers and defenders are equally beside the point. Suffice it to say here that man certainly receives from nature a variety of desires, and that, as a *natural* being, he obeys these. That he should so obey, however, is not for him a necessity; man is also a *rational* being, and *can* receive every particular at the bar of the universal. It is his, then, to raise the desires of nature into motives of reason—to convert them into the rational system of social life, and when he obeys them then, he but obeys his own self. However limited, contingent, subjective, our desires may be, it is certain that they can be freed, articulated, and objectified into an organic whole—Law, Morals, and the State. This is the "*liberty* of a wise *restraint*," this is "the *necessity* in duty that will make us *free*," and the man who knows not so to restrict and restrain himself, will never come to anything. Only he who can accept the limit will ever reach the true illimitable.

This limitation, in fact, is the true concrete will, the particularized universal, will in the moment of singularity (and singularity here has not the meaning of individuality). This, in a word, is the true free-will. For what is this but thinking will—will, then, that wills its own implement, its own self. And it is certain that to be a free being it is only necessary to be a thinking being: the right of freedom is but the privilege of reason. What Hegel calls objective spirit is but the *realization* of free-will—of will, rational will, thinking will, substantiating itself in actual outward fact. *That* actual outward fact is the world of Right, the rational system of observances, legal, moral, and political, into which a community of reasoning beings, by very nature, and that is *by very nature of the notion*, sunders. So, however, will only works itself free from its own individuality—its state of *nature*—emancipates itself *from* nature into reason—realizes itself into the substantial freedom of organized universality. What we have here, in fact, is the great distinction—in a *moral* reference—between subjectivity and objectivity. When I think what is *mine* only, when I do what is *mine* only, I think a mere subjectivity, I do a mere subjectivity, which in *rerum natura*, which in the universe of things, is simply nothing and nowhere and of no account; but when I think and do what *all* in thinking and doing can appropriate and call theirs, then I think and do an objectivity, a concrete and a permanent that actually functions in fact. To such a word as *mine*, subjectivity and objectivity give a double accent. What is *mine* subjectively, as of this special particular passing individual who now speaks, I must *italicize;* but what is MINE objectively, I must write in small capitals; for that mine is MINE as belonging to my essence, which is humanity as humanity, reason as reason. The italicized *mine* is what sunders and separates and isolates us, each from the other, as so many uncommunicating and incommunicable individual distinct atoms; whilst the MINE with a double accent, the MINE in small capitals, is what brings us all together into a concrete unity, into a living universal. And it is here that we can discern our only duty which is to raise subjectivity into objectivity, the contingent individual into the necessary universal. Almost, we might say, our only duty is twice to italicize "mine," or our only duty is in this way to negate the negation. To italicize "mine" once is to set subjectivity, to destroy "mine," really to negate it; but to italicize "mine" twice, is to set objectivity, and negate the negation. Now this is the one object of education—or this is what ought to be that one object; for education is not a mere chattering of vocables. *Nature* is a system of mechanical necessity; every one member of it is in blind interdependence with and on all the rest, and none is for itself. This, too, is the case with man, so far as what is called *nature* in him is concerned. Nature in man, in that sense, is his needs and greeds, and in these man is bound and not free; but there is in him the possibility of freedom: he can reflect, he can retire into his universal and negate nature—nature in the sense that it is the individual particular. Reflection does not remain by the particular that is presented to it, but opposes to it another—opposes to it its own contrary. Now, precisely this is the business proper of education—to rouse reflection, to convert *instinctive* action into *reflective* action, and reflective action into *free* action—into the free action of the *emancipated universal*. So it is that our needs and greeds, our vanities and vainglories, and all that holds of mere nature in us, are controlled—our own essential will, our free-will realized. "Education," says Hegel, "has for object to raise man into a self-dependent being, that is, into a being of free-will. With this intention many restrictions are imposed on the inclinations of children. They must learn to obey, so that their individual or special will in its dependence on sensuous needs and greeds may be sublated, and their true will freed."

In man, then, evidently, there is a possibility that lies not in the lower animals: *his* will *may* be raised from a will of nature, a will of the particular into a will of reason, a will of the universal; but there exists in *this* world no power that could raise *their* wills so. The lower animal is adequate to a *particular* only: its motives are *individual* incitement after *individual* incitement, each of which it only blindly obeys; universal it has none. On the other hand, *it is the single antithesis of universal and particular that makes the whole world of man:* that *cross* is the foundation of his science; that *cross* is the foundation of his law, morals, politics, art; that *cross* is the foundation of his religion. The antagonism that lies in this *cross* is the pulse of history, each beat of which is but the conversion of the lower into the higher. This antithesis or cross has hardly yet been looked at by any man in full consciousness, as it were, with his eyes open, perfectly aware of the importance of what he looked at. Nevertheless, it is the ultimate and absolute secret: it is the *Notion,* the *concrete notion.* No highest philosopher for centuries will have anything to do, but to make this notion *explicit,* bring it into full consciousness. Free-will, as we have seen, is but another name for it, and free-will is but a will according to conscious motives. Those, then, as we have seen already, who have hitherto discussed this question have simply mistaken the hinge on which it turned, whether they supposed themselves to attack, or whether they supposed themselves to defend. It is as erroneous to say on the one side man must act by motive and is bound, as to say, on the other side, man can act without motive and is free. Man *must* act by motive, and it is the very necessity of that *must* that frees him. If man *could* act without motive, he were not free, but bound. It is the existence of conscious motive that proves the existence of the universal, and in the subordination of the particular motive to the universal motive lies freedom. As Hegel points out, then, that man is free because he can do what he likes, is a conception very wide of the mark. In short, man is free because he can not do what he likes: man is free because he must obey motive—man, that is, in reference to the universal in him. Similar blunders are not rare in philosophy. There is subjective idealism, for example. Well, because in the relation of a subject and an object, there is no possible way of the former *knowing* the latter but *within*, it is argued that the latter also must *be* within. That is, the very reasons I allege for knowing an object *without* are used by subjective idealism for *not* knowing an object without. That that alone renders a knowledge of externality possible—the very condition in which that knowledge roots—is used for the annihilation of all possibility of its own progeny! We see the same thing again in regard to a substance and its qualities; a substance can only make itself *known* by its qualities. Such is the temper of the day, that because that is the case, it is supposed to be philosophy to say, though it is only in consequence of its qualities that a substance is *known*, it is also only in consequence of its qualities that a substance is *not* known, and just because it is only in consequence of its qualities that it *is* known! Here again we see the very condition of knowledge is made the very reason of ignorance—the reasoner looking very grave at the result, pulling his collar up, and calling himself a philosopher. As it is in these cases, then, so it is in that of free-will. It is only in consequence of sensation that we *can* know an external world, and therefore, it is only in consequence of sensation that we can*not* know an external world. It is only through qualities that a substance is known, and therefore it is only through qualities that a substance is *not* known. It is only through motives that a free-will is possible, and therefore it is only through motives that a free-will is *im*possible. It is really marvellous how long very respectable men, how long the whole world, will allow itself to be stultified by such transparent hocus-pocus.

It is not moral necessity but moral freedom that we should say of will then; for in truth the necessity of will is the only freedom. All outward things, all things of nature, have their very essence in mechanical necessity; but all inward things again, all things of reason, have their very essence in freedom, and so it is that the two worlds are opposed. Will is universal; there is no object *its* that it does not make its; it can abstract from everything. Will, then, wills its own self, and, therefore, is it free. The will that wills its own self must not be conceived as self-will however. The will that must indulge itself in every motive it wills, is a vain, weak, spoiled, sensuous will, and is generally named self-will, or caprice. That is a will given up to mere *nature*, and is not free but bound. There is a will again which we name *wilfulness;* a will, that is, that will not give up what *it* wills, and for no other reason than that it is *it* wills. Such wilfulness is sometimes regarded as constituting strength of character; but without the universal, it is as weak as the will that I have called *spoiled will*, and certainly, for the most part, far more dangerous. It is neither the indulgence of spoiled will, then, nor the stubbornness of wilfulness that makes freedom; it is only the universal, and in the universal lies the *community* of mankind. *All* take part in an action, *all* approve or disapprove, for each in will feels himself universal, and through that universality reflected in the other. This subject of free-will—which, as has more than once transpired, is the root of law, and which I have been obliged somewhat to lean on as the very principle and centre of the philosophy of law, —this subject cannot be better closed than by a sentence or two direct from Hegel:—

"Of no idea is it so generally known that it is indefinite, ambiguous, liable to the greatest misconstructions, and, in reality, consequently, subjected to them, than of the idea of free-will, and none is in current use with so little intelligence. But, as we may express ourselves, the *free* spirit being the *actual existent* spirit, or the spirit that actually prevails in human affairs being the spirit of free-will, misconstructions in regard to it are of the most enormous consequence; for when persons and peoples are once for all possessed by the abstract notion of freedom as such, freedom on its own account, no other has such irresistible power, and just because it is the very inmost being of spirit,—its very actuality and self. Entire quarters of the globe, Africa, and the East, have never had, and have not yet this idea. The Greeks and Romans, Plato and Aristotle and the Stoics, had it not. On the contrary, they conceived only that a man by his birth (as Athenian or Spartan citizen, &c.), or by strength of character, by education, by philosophy (the wise man is free even when a slave or in chains), only so did they conceive a man to be free. This idea came into the world through Christianity, in which it is that the individual, *as such*, has an *infinite* worth, as being aim and object of the love of God, and destined, consequently, to have his absolute relation to God as spirit, to have this spirit dwelling in him. Christianity it was, namely, that revealed man *in himself* to be destined to supreme freedom . . . . This idea, then, is the very actuality of man, and not that he *has* it, but that he *is* it. *Christianity* has made it the very actuality of its adherents,—the very actuality of its adherents, not to be a slave for example. If reduced to slavery, if the control over their property is to depend on caprice and not on laws and courts of justice, then they find the very substance of their being violated. This volition of freedom is no longer an impulse, an instinct that demands its gratification; it is now *character*,—a spiritual consciousness that is above impulse, that is above instinct. But this freedom, this free-will, and free-agency, that possesses such implement, such filling, such aims and ends, cannot remain as notion only, as mere principle of the mind or the heart; it must unclose itself into objectivity,—into an organic actuality, legal, moral, political, and religious."

This, then, is the position we have now reached: that man, as free-will, is the objective spirit, and must realize himself in the institutions, legal and other, by which society lives. In one word, then, the matter of law is our own free-will, and its existence in the state is but its *realization*. It is the course which this realization, in obedience to its very principle, takes that we have now to see.

Free-will, then, is the root of all, and freedom, liberty, itself must constitute the contents of Right or of Law. But free-will, at first, taken just so, is abstract, is without this development of its contents into its own concrete system—is, as yet, but *notion;* it is not yet *idea.* So it is, as yet, but direct or immediate to itself and us; it is, as yet, but one and single. Thus immediate, direct, single, *one,* it is a *Person.* But free-will is essentially an action, and that action is essentially a movement from within *outwards.* Now, the *nearest* outer to its own self is *another—another person.* The first prescript of Right, then, is, Be a person, and respect others as persons. It is plain also, that in this abstraction there are no other interests present—no variety of concrete interests as under morality. There is no concrete with its various composing members or interests to disturb beside it. There is no interest in question but the single interest of free-will, no command but that will is to be free. But, as between persons, that amounts only to a *prohibition*—obstruct not the free-will of the person. This prohibition is also *categorical;* it gives no reasons for itself; it interposes no conditions; it is categorical, and not hypothetical. It does not require, as is required in morals, the other person to follow it with intelligence, assent, conviction; it never asks for any motive or design, or intention on the part of the other person. It simply says, categorically, Infringe not the free-will of the person, or violate not personality. These consequences really flow directly from the nature of the case. So it is, then, that this division of Right—the first—is but formal, abstract, without any concrete filling, implement of humanity as such. Or personality gives the *capacity* for legal rights; it is the foundation from which all abstract, formal right arises; but even as such, it is only abstractly universal. There is no *particularity* in it, as in morals, no special interest that concerns me as an individual, say. It has no thought of my individual advantage or welfare; and is wholly indifferent to my agreement with it, to my convictions in its regard, or to my designs and intentions in the realization of it. The very abstractness of the universality here has its own limitations, then. To be a person is, in one sense, to be what is highest; but to be a person is to let all our other concrete humanity fall, and be also what is lowest, or, at all events, *least.* So it is that we find the individual who is only a person, the individual who only fixes himself in his *right,* for the most part so thin and narrow. We see, also, that it is generally the rude and unformed man who so stubborns himself in his abstract right, while the richer, fuller nature has an eye for every side of the interest at stake, and has no difficulty in complete resignation of his abstract right. An exalted sense for formal right may prove in the end but mere *wilfulness,* indeed—a formal will, that in its own intensely pure formality, can only remain blind to every concrete consideration beside it. I recollect of a case, indeed, where a poor man nearly ruined himself by the consistency of his faith in formal or abstract right. He was the landlord of a workshop; and the tenant, without consent asked or given, took it upon him to enlarge the old windows in this workshop, and open new ones. The workshop is mine said the landlord, and you have infringed my rights. But what I have done, said the tenant, I have done at my own expense, and what I have done is an improvement to the property. I admit that, said the landlord, but you had no right to make alterations in *my* property without *my* consent, and I will take you to law there-*for.* Accordingly, this landlord did take this tenant to law; he lost his case before judge after judge, and he was just on the point of taking it to the House of Lords, when death kindly stepped in, and by *its* abstraction did justice to *his.* Here was a true instance of exalted devotion to abstract right, but the *concrete* injury did not stop there; for the tenant, disgusted with the doings of the landlord, neglected his business, neglected the property, allowed a valuable boiler to burst, became in the end bankrupt, and left a workshop that was worth a great deal to the *landlord* worth next to nothing to his *heirs.* So much for the worship of formality. The higher nature, then, may, in view of other and more concrete interests, let its formal right fall. And it is very subtle on the part of Hegel to point out, accordingly, that formal right is only a possibility, for a possibility, as he expressly defines it here, "is a *Seyn,* a being, an existent something, that has the import also not to be," and we can see *that* in the interest before us. My abstract right *is,* but how often is it also *not?* as I think it not worth while to assert it. That is, abstract right, beside concreter interests, has only the significance of a possibility, and it has its own felicity when Hegel remarks further, that accordingly, the legal assignment here is only an *Erlaubniss* or a *Befugniss,* which, I suppose, I may translate by *permission* and *title*—the meaning being that such rights may remain empty, and be nothing but a permission *to,* a title *to.* Nevertheless, though such be the dangers of formal or abstract right, the importance of the position must not be lost sight of. Neither individuals nor nations are even *concretely* advanced until they have reached a knowledge of the stage of abstract personality. Such advance must be allowed to have been largely an achievement of the Romans, of whom it may be said, in reference to their legal assignments, that their greatest feat even in the very acme of their development was to perfect this consciousness—to perfect the inviolability of the person as person; for the particular individual, if richer, more concrete, is so mostly on the *natural* side, and it is consideration of the universal individual, the person, that brings freedom. "In personality, indeed, it lies that I, as, on all sides of me, in inward desire, need, greed, and appetition, and in direct outward existence, *this* perfectly limited and finite individual, am yet—as person that is—pure self-reference, and know myself, even in my finitude, as what is infinite, universal, and free."

In abstract Right, then, it is the mere universal will that is considered, without respect of the individual in his further concrete interests, or in his (moral) convictions and intentions: it has no object but the human free agent as such. In short, free-will respects only its own self. Even in the other it respects only its own self. So it is that each is a person, and so it is also that all the *edicts* of law here are *interdicts*—all its positive *commands* are in ultimate instance *inhibitions*. This by reason specially of the very abstractness of the person. I may add here that, if in respecting other persons we respect also ourselves, it is very important to see that in respecting ourselves we respect also them; and this is a profound lesson to that morbid self-contempt that, in these days of loudness and superficiality, is so common in the quieter and the deeper.

But the Person cannot *remain* abstract: he must *realize* his freedom, obtain objective existence for it; the *notion* must become *idea*. So abstractly immediate, so abstractly direct to its own self as will on this stage is—and at the same time so abstractly inner to its own self—for *plurality*, the consideration of *persons*, makes no difference here, each is but *a person*, and as empty and abstract as the other—so abstractly immediate, though inner, then, what different thing will can here realize itself in, will be itself immediately and externally abstract—a thing, an external thing. But for will to realize itself in an external thing is to take *possession* of it—is to enter into its *Property*.

Of course, Gentlemen, you see what all this amounts to. In this mode of statement, when one part of a subject is completed, and it is now necessary to go to a new part, this new part must *introduce itself*, and not be *just turned to*. Thus we saw how, the intellectual powers having been discussed, and the turn of the active powers being now arrived, these latter were not just tacked on to the former, but the former actually *became* the latter. Theory, by a turn of the hand, *became* practice; intelligence, will. Now will, thus come upon, is as yet undeveloped, and so it can be figured as still something *single, one, internal to its own self, abstract*, &c. But will that can be so described *corresponds to the definition* of a Person, and *is* therefore a Person. Again, this abstract personality must *realize* itself, but, being so *abstract* and *internal* itself, the *other*, in which only it can realize itself, must, on *its* side, be *externally* abstract, &c.—that is, an outward material thing—Property. I am not sure that you will yet altogether relish this new mode of proof; but I think you will now see something of its nature.

We have now once for all arrived at Property; and Property, Contract, and Penalty shall be the themes of our two remaining lectures.

LECTURE III.

GENTLEMEN,—In our last lecture, we saw the realization of freewill into a person on the one hand, and property on the other. Freewill itself was the terminal result into which all that held of theory had collapsed,—a result which, simply as that and no more, was necessarily undeveloped. But this undevelopedness gives freewill, as we so have it, a character of singleness and oneness—or this undevelopedness and firstness, so to speak, give it a character of abstractness; for that is abstract—as sweetness, whiteness—that is in isolated self-identity only. And we can see that if whiteness is abstract in consequence of its isolatedness to self, for the same reason the broken-off hand of a watch, or a separated main-spring, is also abstract. In short, any one member of a concrete is, being isolated, abstract: so any one moment of the notion or of *a* notion—the universal, the particular, or the singular—being isolated, is abstract. Freewill, then, as it first emerges, has, being undeveloped, the character of singleness, oneness, and abstractness. But a will, a freewill, single, one, and abstract—that is a person. This personality now must *realize* itself, for if overtly, explicitly abstract, it is also latently, implicitly concrete, and that for no other reason than that it is will—thinking will. But realization takes place always through something else or other; now, to such an abstract *inner*, what can be *other* but a similarly abstract *outer?* and that is an external thing, property.

These considerations are hard, for they are wholly peculiar and wholly new—in this peculiarity and strangeness they may not carry conviction either—still they will be allowed to possess their own subtlety and felicity. Again, it must not escape notice that the machine engaged in the manipulation and working up of all this is the notion: we have but a single substance, a single material, all through, passing from roller to roller of the various moments. Will, coming to us as bare result, is the undeveloped universal that, *in itself*, or implicitly concrete, must strive forward into its correspondent particular, and thence further into its correspondent singular. This is the march everywhere, and, so far at least, we may acknowledge in the person a moment of universality as in property a moment of particularity.

The most common sense passage I can find in Hegel bearing on these points is this:—"All things are capable of being made man's property, because man is freewill, and, as such, in and for himself" (that is, responsible, amenable only to his own self); "but what is opposed to him has not this quality. Every man has the right, then, to set his will in the things of existence, to sublate them, and make them his; for they, as external, have no self-end; they are not the infinite reference of self to self" (which every subject is); "they are even to *themselves* externalities. The lower animals, even, are such externalities, and, so far, things. Only will is infinite, absolute to all else, whilst all else is only relative. To make them mine is at bottom, consequently, only to manifest the dignity of my will as compared with external things, and demonstrate that they are not in and for themselves, or have no self-end. The manifestation itself takes place in this way that I set in the particular thing another end than that which it immediately had. I give to the lower animal another soul than what it had. I give it my soul." It is in this way that Hegel places us in presence of freewill and of an outer world in which it is to realize itself; and he really believes that he never makes a single step in advance without its own *deduction*. We are once for all arrived, then, at the notions of person and property: the one the abstract, self-*in*ternal immediate, the other the abstract, self-*ex*ternal immediate. This word *immediate* I have used before, and it always gives a certain difficulty; but what is separated, isolated, secluded to its own self, what is abstracted (or abstracted from) is something taken out of all its *bemediating* connections and relations, and so therefore something immediate and direct.

Hegel treats the subject of a philosophy of right under the three great divisions of Abstract Right, Morality, and what he calls *Sittlichkeit;* and the principle that guides him in this is, as always and everywhere, the notion. The first division, that is, is but right in its universality; the second, right in its particularity; and the third, right in its singularity. But though such is the succession in Hegel, we are not to suppose that the latter members depend upon the former as earlier in time or superior in dignity. That they are *members* is what we must not allow to escape us, and that the truth consequently is the one concrete whole. Still, for all that, Hegel is not quite without an *historical* consideration here—say, in the transition from abstract law to subjective morality. Law, as treated elsewhere, is very often referred to a moral basis, while here in Hegel, morals, on the contrary, would appear to be referred to a legal basis. Now that is not without a certain *historical* support. It cannot be denied that what Hegel means by morality was represented—fairly represented—nay, very perfectly represented, in the person of Socrates; while what he means by abstract right did not reach full historical development till under the Roman Empire. Still it is not in Socrates, but in Christianity, that Hegel acknowledges the veritable historical first of subjective morality, or the law of conscience, inner righteousness, on the one hand, and of the law of love on the other. And surely these are correct ideas—surely it was only after Christianity that the individual, and not isolatedly, but in connection with the whole community, came to know the full import of what is named moral experience. Christianity it was that wrought as a purifying ferment in the souls of men, abasing all the greeds of sense, shaming the lusts and prides and vanities of self, awakening repentance, chastening the heart, and leading the soul generally into candour and simplicity and humility and love. Now that is precisely the position of subjective morality, and as opposed to abstract right. Under the latter the requisite is only to do the right, no matter whether you agree with it or not, and no matter what your motives, intentions, or general spirit may be. But morality is plainly an internalization of such a standpoint, of such a material. While the standard under law was without, it is now under morality within—it has become conscience. And really the one step may be regarded as having led to the other: only after men had long mechanically and unreflectingly obeyed law did they come to make its prescripts their own principles, did they come to see that these prescripts were but what their own nature, and no mere external authority, commanded. But the moment the faintest edge of such an experience as that was received into the heart, morality had begun. Morality, then, is but a particularization of law, or it is but law in the moment of particularity. Law, namely, as we have seen, is wholly universal. Its prescripts are directed only to the abstract person, only to freewill as freewill. But there is an advance in concretion now: the person has become a subject, or better, a neighbour. And the very word neighbour opens a vista into a sphere of concrete interests infinitely richer and more complicated than that connected with the abstract rights of a person.

What Hegel means by *Sittlichkeit*, again, is a still higher advance in concretion. This word really means simply morality. The *Sitte* is but the Greek ἦθος, the Latin *Mos*, our own *Custom*. What Hegel sees in it, however, is the substantial custom that has sprung from objective reason, and is fixed, established, stereotyped in the conscience and practice of a people. So it is that I translate it *observance*, sometimes *instinctive*, sometimes *substantial observance*. And these words, I think, will pretty well convey the meaning, though it must be confessed that the task of a translator here is excessively puzzling. One *wrong* translation I will refer to. I have seen the word *Sittlichkeit* translated *conventionality*. But that is a mistake. Early in one's studies, no doubt, such a translation has its own temptations; but it is entirely to miss the matter in hand to yield to them. What we mean by conventionalities are temporary customs, mere arbitrary agreements. Thus it is a convention when leaving home and desirous that your friends should call on you when you return, that you pay them a visit to say goodbye, or, in their absence, leave a card for them with P.P.C. —*pour prendre congé*—written on it. That is a convention. Again, it used to be a custom that when the representatives of a family made their periodical and ceremonious call on another family, the gentleman in handing in the card for himself and wife, bent in a corner of it with his thumb. Now that is something purely and simply conventional. But such conventionality is very remote indeed from the Hegelian *Sitte.* By it we are to understand something not subjective but objective, not contingent but necessary, not arbitrary but rational—something fixed, permanent, established—something looked upon as sacred and springing from a sacred source. I have tried all manner of English words for it, and once thought I had got over the difficulty by translating *Sittlich, Sittlichkeit,* and *Sitte,* respectively by the terms *ritual, rituality,* and *rite,* but had to give them up too, what they suggested being either too ecclesiastical or too externally ceremonial. Were we to reserve the Latin *morality* for Hegel's *Moralität,* and the Greek *ethicality* for Hegel's *Sittlichkeit,* the end so far would be pretty well attained, but we should still want a word for *Sitte.* It is this word *Sitte* that I propose to render by *observance,* and I really have been quite unable to find any single English term that would suit better. Could we use *custom*—the commonest term of all—that indeed would be preferable, but I think your ears will tell you that that is impossible, at all events at first.

If we consider it well, there is an abstractness, a one-sidedness observable in will, whether as manifested in right, or as manifested in morality; whereas in observance will is concrete, and any such defect disappears. In right, for example, will is realized in something merely external, while in morality again it is realized only internally in the contingent individual subject. This is not so, however, in regard to the *Sittlich,* the observational, where what is inner is also outer, and what is outer is also inner. Take filial obedience, for example, *there* is a *Sitte,* a sacred usage, a civil custom, a substantial observance, and we can see it to be no less real as an outward act than as an inward sentiment, and no less real as an inward sentiment than as an outward act. Societary usage that is as well societary sentiment, or societary sentiment that is as well societary usage, —that, then, is *Sittlichkeit,* that then, is *observance.* In such usage we see society to be in enjoyment of what we may call the second or higher nature; such usage, or the system of such usages, we can see also to be capable of being named the substance of freewill, a substance which each individual freewill, each member of the society knows to be that individual member's own proper substance. *He* then possesses virtue, ethical personality, whose whole nature is permeated and pervaded by this substantial life, who regards accordingly his particular place in the system as not negative to him, but peacefully accepts it, trusting implicitly in the whole, and ready to sacrifice himself to it; and this is so, not as regards the State only, but as regards every one of its subordinate particular institutions.

We see, then, the nature of Hegel's threefold division of the science of right, and we see more particularly that this division has been prescribed by the notion. The first division, abstract right, or what we may call legality, is will in the universality of the person; the second, morality, is will in the particularity of the neighbour; and the third, *Sittlichkeit*, ethicality, or we may even say politicality, is will in the singularity of the citizen or political subject. Of course the series, legality, morality, politicality, as well as the series, person, neighbour, citizen, can only correspond to the series universality, particularity, singularity, when the words of each are precisely understood as Hegel understands them. Understood as we understand them, *person, neighbour*, for example, are perhaps each less universal than *citizen*. Both words, indeed, neighbour and citizen, are, as used here, my own, and there must be seen in them only Hegel's notions. The same principle that conditions the general classifications conditions also the subordinate ones, and when legality or abstract right is divided into Property, Contract, and Penalty, it is still the march of the notion through its moments that Hegel sees and would have us see. What respects form, however, will perhaps be still more intelligible when we draw into preciser consideration the matter discussed.

The essence of property, as we have seen, then, is that a physical object—an object without will—is transformed from its own brute externality and meaninglessness into an embodiment of free will. In property, accordingly, there is a union of two factors; of free will on the one hand, and of an external object on the other, and this union is as necessary to the one as to the other. If the object acquires meaning and function only when it is taken up into the life of the person, this person, for his part can become manifestible only through the object. Singly and in disunion either element is abstract, only in union, only together are they both concrete. From this, then, we see at once the tautology of the prescript that what I can take as property must be *res nullius; that va sans dire;* for what already expresses free will is already my will, and no longer an alien object that only waits embodiment. Again the will, as we have it in the person, is, as has already been discussed, very evidently single; what it takes into possession must be single also. It cannot take possession, then, of genera, or of the elements. The person, in his singleness, cannot take possession of the genus vegetable or of the element air. Being single, he cannot make private property of what is universal. Even to make good his right of community in what is universal, this universal itself must be converted into singles, as into breaths of air and draughts of water. We are to perceive here then, that it is the nature of the person rather than that of the object that is the dictating element; just as it is this person's will, and not the fact merely of his being *first*, that enables him to make anything his. It would be idle for freewill to make its what were already its; and to make mine what is his is to negate freewill, is to negate my own will. For property is an absolute assignment, and no mere result of mutual agreement. *This* is not *mine* simply because of my acknowledgment that *that* is *yours*. This is mine, that is yours, because freewill as freewill has set itself into either. Freewill is embodied in property, and through property is the intercourse of freewill with freewill mediated. But as this is so, or as it is the possession of property that gives objective reality to my freewill, it is my duty to possess property—property, I say, and not such and such property. What and how much property I may possess are not considerations that belong to our present sphere, where we are confined to the abstract right of the person. Of that person, however, it is certainly not only the right, but also the duty, to be a possessor of property. And here I may point out the importance of the lesson indicated. It used to be very much the fashion to run down riches and cry up poverty—especially wherever and whenever it was supposed that the young were in hearing. The bliss of poverty and the bale of riches—this was set us in every copy line. No page of any primer but was sonorous with it, and it was rounded into our ears in every new tongue we came to—Latin, or Greek, or French, or German. We heard it in Church too, just as we heard it at home, or as we heard it in school. And when we came to the University we were assured by the Professor of Morals that that was philosophy—that that was wisdom. Then we read it in the ancients and we read it in the moderns: Cicero and Horace and the seven wise men, Simonides and Phocylides and the rest, were for ever talking of it, and even in these very days our last great man asserted, as by an authority *de par le roi*, that if he had a true man to bring up, with the heart of a man in him, he would say rather let him be poor! It may seem very bold then, should I at all hint disagreement here with an opinion that has been so long, so variously, and so authoritatively sanctioned. Nevertheless, it does seem to me that the effects of this opinion have not been always good. I fear that too many a bright young literary soul has been led away by it, despising money as money, and undervaluing the honest industry that was to bring it, marrying improvidently, living *au jour le jour*, believing that every mouth brought its own bite with it, and trusting quite unmisgivingly to the future, till having piped his best all his summer of youth like the grasshopper, he was refused food by the ants and told only to dance his best in the winter of his old age. Of course, I would not for a moment have it supposed that I take the opposite extreme, and counsel the pursuit of riches as man's sole business. These very days of ours are not less full of the futility of that vulgarity than of the disappointment and regret that are the end of the former delusion. What I have only to point out here is that it is the duty of man as man to possess property. In truth no man is a man till he is also a proprietor. Then it is only that he has entered into the concrete life of the state, and is of any true value—then it is only that he has attained life—a concrete life for himself. He is a person now, a citizen, a neighbour; no nerve or artery of the whole but meets in him; he lives the whole and enjoys the whole, and feels in short that only now properly can he say that he lives at all. How different the young literary enthusiasts who will not make money, but will only pipe! These, after all, live only an abstract life, and they feel themselves in the end, not as their fellows, but isolated and apart, lonely, useless, miserable. This, then, is the lesson here, that it is about the first duty of manhood to respect property, knowing that only through property does a man enter into the state and become one with the concrete. So it will be advisable that all those young literary enthusiasts who threaten to live only abstract lives should undergo apprenticeship in a lawyer's office. There probably sooner than anywhere else will they be brought to sanity as regards property.

It is the duty, then, of every freewill, of every person, to possess property; and so far all freewills, all persons, are *equal*. And here it is we get the true light on that equality that is so current among certain political parties now-a-days. All human beings, that is, in so far as they are persons, are not only free but equal. Equality and freedom are by no means convertible terms however; they are not even in direct, but rather in inverse proportion. Hegel's own expressions in this reference are among his happiest and most exoteric, and I think you will not ask me to beg pardon for following them here pretty closely.

Hegel commences by admitting that it is not incorrect to regard the main interests of a constitution as centring in what the words Freedom and Equality imply; but he complains that, as generally used, they are abstract and can only lead to the destruction of the concrete that the state is. This concrete itself, the state, is precisely what on one side introduces inequality and must introduce inequality; for the distinctions of rulers and subjects, of ranks and classes, of authorities and of those amenable to these, are inseparable from it. To carry equality rigorously out then would be to put an end to these and the state itself. Then it is said all men are equal by nature; but it is quite plain that when physical nature is meant all men are rather unequal by nature; while, by nature the notion being meant, all men are indeed so far equal, but not to the exclusion of infinite inequality otherwise. That we should be pronounced equal as persons, as men—and not as in Greece and Rome because we happen to be certain men, and not certain other men—this is not the product of nature but of the consciousness of the deepest principle in our spiritual structure, and of the long and laborious evolution of this consciousness into its present universality. Again, as said, equality as persons does not exclude infinite inequality otherwise. That all citizens are equal before the law has no extension beyond that legal equality of the person. Otherwise, or the person apart, we are not more equal before the law than away from the law. It is precisely according to that inequality away from the law that the law itself indeed taxes us. In regard to taxes plainly, it would be monstrous injustice in the law to regard us all as equal, though, at the same time, it must and can be led only by what it sees equal in us in regard to property, age, ability, sex, &c.

As regards freedom again it ought not to be taken abstractly as the freedom of subjective self-will. Legal restriction ought to be seen to be the true freedom; and formerly, precisely such restrictions used to be called *the* freedoms, *the* liberties. In effect, every veritable law is a freedom, a liberty, for it is a result of objective reason. In the best sense, it is not true, then, that the state is but the mutual limitation of each other's liberties; in the best sense, on the contrary, the state is a realization of liberty; for in reality to restrain particular or formal will is to emancipate universal and substantial will. We see but a similar mistake when it is said too, that modern nations are more susceptible of equality than liberty; what is in question here is but abstract equality and abstract liberty, and it is only right that abstract presuppositions in regard to liberty, as these are, should be found to *break* on the realm of reality and fact as more rational and powerful in its concretion than they in their abstraction. It is more correct in this reference to say, on the contrary, that the high development of the modern state introduces the greatest concrete individual *inequality;* while, on the other hand, the deeper rationality and the firmer stability of the laws lead to a proportionally greater liberty, which also they can more readily concede and endure. The very word liberty moreover implies a certain antithesis to equality, and the more firmly established liberty is as the security of person and property, as opportunity to develop and make available talent and other advantages, the less there is of equality, and the more of liberty itself even in a subjective sense, as that of the will of the individual.

These are excellent reflections, Gentlemen, and they readily suggest important applications. It is that cry of equality that is the dominant phenomenon of the day now, and we may understand it in its true light by the assistance of these observations of Hegel. The workmen find themselves as good as their masters, the servants as their mistresses, our wives as their husbands, and they all cry equality, meaning only an abstract identity that is utterly impossible. So much does the cry continue extending, nevertheless, that we may presently expect to meet a demand for the equality of children with parents, or to hear the tailor complain that it is very unjust he should be a tailor, the dancing-master similarly rebel against his vocation, and grocers and haberdashers and linen-drapers, and even perhaps lawyers *and* lecturers—all complain that they are very ill-used individuals, and insist on the original identity which is their birthright. That word *identity*, indeed, mirrors the whole matter, and we simply see that the *differences* are tired of being differences, and would fain sink to rest together in the negation of the blank identity which were the only equality. In short, it is the old story of the revolt of the members, the state being substituted for the belly as that that is to be destroyed. It seems indeed to be the creed of the highest enlightment now-a-days that what is called a state is but an expensive superfluity; that society, civilization, is nothing but the raising of commodities and the exchange of them, and that no control is required there but that of the policeman to keep the workman quiet. Accordingly, with this end in view, we are exhorted to doctor and parson ourselves, and I suppose I may add, lawyer ourselves and lecture ourselves. If we would cure the evil, we must cure it in the root, however, that is we must quash the raising of commodities itself; for it is quite certain that from that root the whole ramified and overshadowing calamity springs. To raise a single commodity, taking the commodity as a commodity, and not as a single cabbage or a single potato, supposes the whole iniquitous system, supposes workmen and food and clothes and ships and railroads and steam-engines—supposes science, and all the rest in short; and all the rest, as the concrete differences, can only be kept together in the single concrete identity, in the single concrete life that is the state. Common sense would seem to suggest, then, that we should be far better employed in telling the story of Menenius now-a-days, than in exhorting the hands not to carry and the teeth not to chew.

In further connection with the subject of equality, Hegel refers to the proposal of an equal division of property, and convicts its "emptiness and superficiality" from the very nature of the case. "Not only external nature in its contingency but the entire round of spirit in its infinite individual developments, though under a rational organic whole, falls into *particularity*;" and in saying as much, Hegel intimates that existence, whether physical or metaphysical, must obey the law that lies in the moment of the notion named the *particular*, and inequality is inevitable—not only so, that is, but we must thankfully see it to be so, and that it is only "an empty superficial *understanding*" which, in its abstractions, can blind itself to it. It is but the same blind understanding, too, that complains of the injustice of nature in the inequality of her distributions; for nature, as without freedom, is neither just nor unjust. As for its being the right of every man to have a sufficiency, Hegel remarks, that this, so vaguely spoken, "is only a well-meant, but, as what is well-meant generally is, non-objective moral *wish*, the question at all of sufficiency besides not falling to be discussed under property, but under civil society." It is but in harmony with such views that we find Hegel referring to the Agrarian laws and pointing to the triumph—though at some cost to right otherwise—of the more rational moment in the struggle that took place in their regard between public and private property in land. Family Pacts and *Fidei commissa* in the same connection, Hegel also mentions here as opposed to the right of personality and consequently to that of property. In regard to Plato's republic, he remarks that it fails in the moment of particularity, and is unjust to the person in making him incapable of private property; and as for pious benevolent brotherhoods for a community of goods, we are told that such an idea may present itself without difficulty to a moral imagination that misunderstands the nature of right, free-will, of spirit, in its moments, and reminds us that Epicurus objected to some friends of his who had made such proposals that, in the moral and religious reference, they are bad, for they manifest mistrust, and those who mistrust each other are not friends. Further, observes Hegel, "the equality which might be introduced as to distribution of goods, would, depending as these do on industry, speedily dissolve itself again. But what is not to be done, neither shall it be tried to be done. For men are indeed equal, but only as persons, only as regards the principle of possession. By virtue of that principle it is the duty of every one to possess property. If we will speak of equality, this, then, we must regard as the only one. But the question of particularity, what and how much I may possess, that belongs elsewhere; and the allegation is false that right demands equality of property for all of us, for right demands only that each of us shall have property. Rather it expressly is in particularity that inequality has its place, and equality there were unright." In short, private property is a necessity of reason. Free-will must realize itself; that is, necessarily in an outer as outer. Will as will is also singular or individual. Property, therefore, is personal, is *this* particular property, is mine—is this particular property of this particular me. "Seizure is the enunciation of the judgment that a thing is mine. My will has subsumed it—given it that predicate of mine. It is the right of will so to subsume in itself all external things whatever, for it is in itself the universal, while they, not referent of themselves to themselves, are only under necessity and not free. It is in right of this relation that man takes to himself all outer things, and makes of them other things than they are. He treats them so only in accordance with their veritable nature." Hegel considers this to be the case even as regards the body and life itself: those, "like all other things," he says, "I possess only *in so far as it is my will*," and he adds "the brute cannot mutilate or put an end to itself; only man can; the brute has itself indeed in possession; its soul possesses its body; but it has no right to its own life, because it does not will it." Of course, if it is as will-less that external things are capable of being taken into possession, the same reason applies to the lower animals, and we may reconcile ourselves to the whole position, it being premised as necessary and indispensable condition that there shall be no cruelty, that they shall be with us happier even than they would have been with nature. As for the putting of them to death, that, so far as it is only that, is not cruelty. An animal reflects not, it knows nothing of death, thinks nothing of death: its life is as it were infinite, an infinite affirmation, for of the two negatives, birth and death, between which this affirmation hangs, it knows nothing; its life, consequently, is fairly infinite, and death is no diminution to it. How different with us!

> "We look before and after,
> And pine for what is not:
> Our sincerest laughter
> With some grief is fraught:
> Our sweetest songs are those that tell of saddest thought."

Man's life alone of all below is to its own self a life of limitation, a life of finitude: all other lives, even those of what is inorganic, if we may figure its existence so, are to their own selves infinite; for to their own selves they begin not, and neither do they end. Strange too, it is the very finitude of them that makes their infinitude; it is man's very infinitude—the infinitude of his thought—that makes the finitude of his life. And this may be regarded as, in its way, an argument for the immortality of the individual soul; only such immortality were justice to man; for the privilege of reason is but a privilege of pain.

To Hegel, then, even the body, nay, the mind itself, requires to be taken possession of to become in actuality ours. Culture, education, is required for both. The body, in the immediacy of its existence, is inadequate to the soul, and must be *made* its ready organ and its animated tool. The mind, too, is at first, as it were, immersed in nature, and requires enfranchisement. "This enfranchisement is in each subject the *hard labour* against mere subjectivity of action, and against the immediacy of appetite, as against the subjective vanity of feeling and the arbitrariness, or caprice, of self-will. But through this labour it is that subjective will attains to objectivity and becomes capable and worthy of being the *actuality of the idea.* For so particularity is wrought into universality, and through universality becomes the concrete singular."

My body, as mine, must be to another sacred, then, for violence is done my will when violence is done my body. *My* freedom is my body's freedom, and I cannot be degraded into a beast of burden. It is this immediacy of body to mind that makes the difference between an offence to the person and an offence to one's more external property. As regards monstration of possession, the human shape divine is for personality alone ample credentials and authenticity enough; but it is otherwise in regard to external things generally; for the possession of which monstration is indispensable. It is only children, as Hegel points out, who allege bare will as proof of property and as against monstration; and it is certainly not uncommon to find one child trying to prevent another from seizing something by calling out, "It's mine." Mere will will not suffice men, however; for them monstration of some kind is imperatively necessary and rationally so, for an outward objectivity can alone guarantee the inward subjectivity. The setting of will in an object is certainly the notion of property, but there is required also a realization of this.

Seizin, seizure, occupation, possession, or the taking into possession, appropriation, &c.—the mode of this varies and must vary according to infinite conditions bearing on the nature of the object and the power of the individual. As a general rule, it may be said that the more I introduce formation into anything, the more I make it mine. It does not follow, however, that so to speak only *mine* in it is mine, that is, that the form alone is mine. If the form is mine so also is the matter, and it is a mere idle subtlety on the part of Fichte to suggest that the gold cup which I have made a cup is only my cup, and that it is another's to take the gold if he can. Truly, if he can! A substance without qualities is an empty abstraction, and for the rest it is in the substance that I have set my will, and the formation is only a sign thereof. In such cases there is really nothing, then, that, as masterless, another may take. Hegel treats the whole subject of possession under the three heads of Seizure, Use, and Alienation, and affects still to see in this the moments of the notion. We may say, for example, that the affirmation of will in an object corresponds to the moment of simple apprehension, while will that only uses an object only *negates* it—a process, as it were, of judgment, and will that alienates an object returns out of externality into its own self, which may be regarded so far as a moment of reason. For I may remark here, as I have remarked already, in the manipulation of the moments, it is often a convenience to substitute the concreter moments of simple apprehension, judgment, and reason, for the more abstract ones of universality, particularity, and singularity—a substitution for the rest, that throws its own light on the nature of the general ideas involved, which, however, I hope my first lecture demonstrated at full. To correlate seizure, use, and alienation with the moments of the notion, is, nevertheless, I fear, somewhat forced—a remark that must be extended perhaps to Hegel's immediate division here of Appropriation into Bodily Seizure, Formation, and Designation. In that triplet Hegel also affects to see an adumbration of the moments of the notion, and points out that they are—which indeed they are—a rise in generalization, a rise from individuality to universality.

I know not that it is worth while for me to enter at length into all that may be said on these three forms of appropriation. Knowing that I have to say so much in these lectures that is hard to understand, there is a certain temptation to expatiate on what at length will prove universally intelligible, and so get credit, as it were, for having said something at last; but it appears to me to belong far more nearly to my duty to occupy myself rather with what is difficult, and so do at least some actual work in the way of explanation. Of the natural limitations of *bodily seizure*, of its extension by inference to what is in connection with the amount seized, or of its extension in actual fact through artificial means—of all that I think I need say nothing, for a little reflection will suggest it to every one. As regards what is referred to as *connections*, for example, there are conterminous rivers, seas, lakes, pastures, and hunting-grounds—there are rocks and minerals—there are alluvial deposits, strandings, and wreckings, waifs and strays, flotsam, jetsam, game, &c. As concerns such things, it is the *understanding* that decides with its *grounds* and *counter-grounds*, and not the notion with its moments of reason.

What concerns *formation* is as exoteric as what concerns bodily seizure, and may be perfunctorily passed with quite as little scruple. It is evidently a more perfect form of monstration as a more permanent and complete one. The cultivation of the soil, the planting of trees, the raising of cattle must all be regarded as instances of it. The protection of game may also be regarded as a species of formation, and so also may the pasturing, hunting, and fishing of nomads, or other people that come and go, though, so far as monstration is concerned, they are less perfect. I add also that no formation can make a slave, can make property of a human being; and the reason lies not in any expediency of the understanding, but in reason itself, in the notion: man is free-will, and must be respected as such. It is to be allowed, however, that in certain past times, slavery was not so wholly unjustifiable, so far, that is, as many men then had not yet taken possession of themselves, had not yet formed themselves into free-will, but were, so to speak, in mere undeveloped externality and naturality, creatures simply of instinct and brute nature. Now, however, that the seat of industry is the ethical state, slavery is no longer possible, for the ethical state is but the realized idea of liberty.

As for the remaining mode of occupancy, *designation*, or the employment of signs, it is pleasant to see that such a man as Hegel, even with such an infallible touchstone and test in hand as the notion, must have had considerable difficulty in deciding as to what he was to say of it, whether he was to say that it was more perfect or less perfect than the others. Understanding—and with all the mooning madness that his unintelligible dialect and dialectic have attached to him, Hegel's understanding is really about the toughest and soundest going—understanding seems to have led him to say, in the first instance, as to his pupils at Nürnberg, that "occupancy by mere designation of the object is imperfect." And really the attachment of a mere sign—some mere badge, some mere ticket, to an article, appears at first sight about the most partial, perishable, and feeble way of seizing that one can well imagine. So it is we find Hegel remarking in those Nürnberg days:—"The sign, token, or ticket, that does not constitute, as formation does, at the same time the thing itself, is an object that has a signification which lies not in its own nature, but is foreign to it, while, on the other hand, that which is signified again has a nature alien to *its* nature. Designation is therefore arbitrary. What a thing shall be the sign of, is more or less a matter of convenience." Even in the text of the *Rechtsphilosophie*, something of hesitation as to the relative ranks of the three modes of seizure still unmistakably betrays itself. There bodily seizure is spoken of as "on the sensuous side the completest mode, though otherwise only subjective, temporary, and restricted." "Formation" is called "the seizure the most adequate to the idea, as bringing to unity in itself both the subjective and the objective element." Nay, in the *Rechtsphilosophie*, it is directly said of designation itself, that it is "very indefinite." It is in what are called the *Zusätze*, the additions after his death from public lectures, as supplied by students or his own manuscripts, that we find Hegel at last doing designation the justice of acknowledgment which he had all along done it of position: it was always third. There he points out the rise in generalization represented by the three modes in their relative places, which I have already alluded to; characterizes designation as essentially intellectual, and therefore easily applicable to an entire whole; and finally concludes thus:—"Occupancy by means of designation is the most perfect of all, for the other kinds of it are also more or less of the nature of a sign. When I seize a thing, or form a thing, the ultimate import is always a sign that, to the exclusion of others, I have set my will in the thing. The notion of a sign is namely this, that a thing does not stand for what it is, but for what it signifies. A cockade signifies, for example, the nationality of a man, though the colour has no connection whatever with the nation, and exhibits not itself but the nation. By this, that he can give a sign, and by its means acquire, man shows his sovereignty over things."

Here, then, we see that Hegel is led to the truth at last, even by his own notion; for there is no doubt but that designation, as intellectual, is the preferable mode of seizure. Thus it is that the mark, the token, the ticket, however *in*significant, becomes significant. It is a great help and a welcome encouragement to us poor mortals, however, to see our own weaknesses and hesitations reflected in a Hegel, and to know thus that we possess a common nature even with him.

The transition from seizure to use is very characteristic of Hegel, and, of course, accomplished through the *notion*. It is impossible to express this better than Hegel does; but unfortunately it is also impossible to find direct equivalents in English for Hegel's German terms. I must content myself with some faint adumbration of it. In seizure, will has made a thing *its*. The will is thus as it were *positive* in the relation, and the thing *negative*. But the will thus particularly determined by the thing is will in a particular volition, or particular will in a desire, and the negative thing further is at the same instant determined as only *for it* and *serving* it, *ministering* to it. We have thus a particular will *using* a particular thing. If any one will take the trouble to analyze this, he will find that our last result has simply been put into the power of the Notion as so much material to grind—which it accomplishes through its successive rollers of the universal, the particular, and the singular moments. The illustration of Hegel's general procedure, and the source and true nature of its figurativeness contained here, is, as it appears to me, exceedingly telling.

The definition of use that is evidently the consequent result is this:—"Use is the realization of my desire through the alteration, destruction, consumption of the thing, the selflessness of whose nature is thus manifested, and which accordingly accomplishes thus its destiny." Hegel is said to have exclaimed once at table when the dishes were long of coming, "Only let them come—we will soon achieve on them their own destiny." He must, plainly, have had then in mind this sentence of his own composition.

Hegel remarks of use that it is the *real* side of property, and that the perception of this lies at the bottom of the pretext put forth often in cases of wrongful occupation, that what is so occupied was unused. Nevertheless he decides that property is the universal, use the particular, and that, in the *first* instance, it is the former must be deferred to. Still he observes further, that formation, designation, &c., are in themselves *external*, unless will, actually present, give them meaning and value. Property, then, become masterless, as devoid of actual will, may be lost or acquired, in lapse of time, through prescription—which has thus a philosophical basis, and not one of mere expediency. For will to have, it is necessary for will to manifest itself. National monuments are national property, so long as the national honour and memory live in them: when these cease, they become the prey of him who likes. The extinction of copyright depends on the same principle, though in an inverse manner: literary productions become in lapse of time a universal property, and pass into contingent private possession. Mere *land*, as burying ground, or otherwise privileged to non-use, involves a simply arbitrary unactual will, by infringement of which no veritably real interest is injured, and respect for which, therefore, cannot be guaranteed. Hegel has several very fine observations here on attempted distinctions between property and use, on partial and temporary use, value, &c.; but at present I can only refer you to them. It is in this connection that he remarks, "It is more than fifteen hundred years since the liberty of the person through Christianity began to flourish, and became a universal principle for a part—a small one indeed—of the human race. The liberty of property, however, has only since yesterday, we may say, been here and there recognized as a principle. An example from universal history of the length of time required by Spirit for its advance in self-consciousness—and a rebuke to the impatience of foolish opinion."

LECTURE IV.

GENTLEMEN,—The last subject of consideration with us was the alienation of property through long omission of the manifestation of will in it. There the omission was indirect, and the step from indirect to direct omission constitutes the transition from the subject of the use of property to that of its alienation proper. A thing is mine when it is willed mine, and not mine, consequently, when it is willed not mine; or, from that into which I have set my will, I can also withdraw it again. This is alienation which may be an act direct, explicit, and declared, as well as one indirect, implicit, and undeclared. What is alienable, however, must be by very nature *external;* whereas, what is by very nature *internal,* is also by the very terms inalienable. I cannot *outer* what is wholly and solely *inner.* Now, such is my personality as personality; such my freewill, my moral sense, my religious conviction. These I cannot commit to the disposal of another; for they are my very inmost being, my very principle of existence, my very self; and the nature of one's absolute self is freewill, and that is freedom, liberty. I can neither *be* a slave then, nor *have* a slave. All compulsion is unlawful, *but that of law itself,* which, properly considered, is no compulsion; for it is the restoration of right, of freewill, not only to him who has been compelled, but to him who has been the compeller. Or, to put it otherwise, no man can be *compelled,* but to *undo* his *compulsion,* which evidently is the restoration of his own right. He who gives into the possession of another his capability of rights, his moral and religious principles, gives away what he does not possess. Let him once possess them, let him once take his own freewill into possession, and such alienation is impossible. Retrocession from an immoral covenant, then, is no wrong, for the right that might be said to be wronged, as regards either contracting party, no matter which, never could have been his. The inviolable inner of my being is no externality, and once I have taken it into my possession as such, every externality is powerless against it. Nevertheless, a part is, as in relation to the whole, external; and I may alienate to another the *temporary* and *partial* use of my inner abilities. Were such alienation not partial, but complete, then I were again a slave. This question of partial alienation of what is in its nature inward leads Hegel to speak of right in reference to the various products of mind, and one remark here is this: "The merely negative, but indispensably *first*, furtherance of the arts and sciences is to secure those who work in them from theft, and allow them the protection of their property, just as it was the indispensably first, and the most important, furtherance of trade and industry to procure them safety from robbery on the roads." Hegel, naturally also, considers here the question of *self*-alienation, of the alienation of one's life, of suicide. The complete totality of our external activity, life, is not to the personality which it naturally constitutes an outer thing; it is not my right to seek death, then, unless at call of the ethical universal in which I am held, and which is my substance. "Suicide," says Hegel, "may be possibly thought bravery, but it is the false bravery of tailors and girls." Still he seems a little *soft* to the suicides of *the heroes*. "When Hercules burns himself," he says, "when Brutus falls on his sword, that is the bearing of the hero to his own personality; but when the question is of the simple right of suicide, it must be denied to the heroes as well as to the rest." The prohibition here, however, hardly seems a strong one, seeing that it appears to be admitted that there *is* an heroic bearing to which personal life *is* an externality.

Property, as external, is in connection with other things external, which are also properties; but the principle of property is will, and property to property is consequently will to will. This relation of will to will is the true and proper element in which freewill has existence; and property, no longer through subjective will and an external object, but property through a common will, through the will of another—this is the sphere of Contract. And, perhaps, there is that in this transition which will reveal to you at last how the triplet Property, Contract, and Penalty, is conditioned by the moments of the Notion. In property, for example, the relation is that of a *single* will, in contract that of *several* wills, and in penalty that of the common or *universal* will. Very plainly then, there is here but the ordinary succession of the moments, singular, particular, and universal; and I may remark in this connection, that Hegel does not tie himself down to the universal being always first, but allows it freely to exchange places with the singular.

The main moments with Hegel in his treatment of contract are the act of will which constitutes it—from the very notion, and that the realization is a simple consequence of this act, and necessarily contained or implied in it. "My promise in the case of a contract," he says, "implies that I, with my own will, have excluded something from the sphere of what is *mine*, and at the same time, that I have acknowledged that the other person has received it into the sphere of what is *his*. The thing, then, by virtue of the contract, is already the property of the other, inasmuch as, that a thing is mine, so far as it depends on me has its ground in my will. In so far, then, as I should not render to the other the matter of the contract, or fail to put him in possession of it, I should be infringing *his* property. The contract itself binds me to its realization."

There is that in the relation of the mutual wills present in contract which is peculiarly interesting to Hegel. He sees in it all the features of the notion, and so, as he is fain to believe, its sanction also. He finds property an affair of *wills* now, and no longer to depend for manifestation on an *external object.* Contract, he says, is "the process in which there is exhibited and resolved the contradiction that I *am* and *remain* independent proprietor, excludent of the other will, so far as, in a will identical with the other will, I *cease* to be a proprietor." I not only *can*, but *must* alienate property; for it lies in its very notion, that will should be made objective, external. But if it is external it is *another*—that is another will, as it were; and so we have the unity of *different* wills—a unity in which this difference is at once negated and affirmed. This, however, is the very movement of the notion,—the identification of differences, the differentiating of identity—and signifies the production of an identical will in the absolute difference of independent proprietors, in which each, with his own will and with the will of the other, *ceases* to be a proprietor, *remains* a proprietor, and *becomes* a proprietor. It follows, then, that each issues from contract the same proprietor that he entered into it, or that there is virtually between them an *identical* property, this is the *value* in which the articles of the contract are, with all their specific external differences, equal to each other. So it is, says Hegel, that a *læsio enormis* cancels the obligation of a contract. It is in this neighbourhood also that Hegel censures the unilateral and bilateral and other divisions of contract in Roman law—accusing them of superficiality and confusion.

Possession stands to Property as in a relation of substantiality to externality. Property, namely, is an assertion of will, of which possession is the internal reality. This same relation but repeats itself in contract in its two terms of agreement and fulfilment (*præstatio, solutio*). The agreement is wholly substantial, it is in the element of ideality; and the utterance of ideality—expression—is the sign. So the agreement brings itself through the *stipulation,* in the symbolical formalities of gestures or of speech (which last is the fittest expression of ideality) into a sign. The stipulation, therefore, gives an outer body to the ideality of the agreement. Formalities, doubtless, get simpler and simpler; still, for the conversion of subjectivity into objectivity, an externality is necessary, and formalities of some kind will remain *as* necessary for the expression of will, as speech generally for the expression of thought—it lying in these very words that the expression of will will reduce itself more and more to the expression of thought as such. The formalities of contract, then, are not there only to bring a fee to officials, but that the mobile inwardness of will may be stereotyped in an outward and undeniable form. It is impossible to gainsay the value, in all cases, *of the external proof:* a thousand witnesses to the contents of a letter are really impotent beside production of the letter itself. Where agreement and prestation are not simultaneous, then, the stipulation must be regarded as a real essential. What is *implicitly meant* must be *explicitly set.* The derivation of the word *stipulation,* as an outer expression to an inward will, does not seem quite certain. Kant derives it from *stipula:* the contracting parties broke a straw between them. Dr. D. C. Heron, again, has it that "whatever was firm was termed a *stipulum* by the ancients: probably from *stipes,* the trunk of a tree."[1] The stipulation is the guarantee, then, that something does not lie only *in* the will, but actually is willed, and so lies *out* of will—a fact. The stipulation further, then, must be regarded as what in contract is legally *substantial,* or in the stipulation the transfer of property must be regarded as virtually accomplished. This is the declaration of the notion; but, of course, between the stipulation and the prestation there is allowed the usual latitude of *understanding:* understanding has always the fact of the equal *value*—in regard to what is given and what is taken—as basis and standard. Stipulation, moreover, as *substantial,* only applies to what is *substantial*—value. A contract is not a mere promise; and the stipulation gives shape and fixture to the difference. Fichte and others are quite wrong, then, in assuming the obligation in contract only to begin with the beginning of the prestation. Contract is an affair of legal, not of moral right, and has nothing to do with the secret intentions, the state of mind morally, of either side. Duplicity of moral meaning is not allowable in contract, and the stipulation is the embodied and undeniable guarantee of that. Prestation is but the inevitable result of stipulation, and that there are contracts—loans, deposits, &c.—in which agreement and prestation are simultaneous is no proof to the contrary.

As regards the classification of contracts Hegel differs but little from Kant, and as it may be readily found by reference I shall not spend time in its exposition.

Hegel points out that in contract will is not will *as such,* not *absolute* will, but, as limited to, included in, an outer object—so to speak transformed to it—is only formal will, individual will, self-will. That is, in contract the will is but natural will, the object but a natural object, and there is no necessity of reason between them: the will *may* express itself in the object, but it may also withdraw itself again. In contract, then, the wills are self-wills, natural, individual wills; the one will that results is only one of community, and not of substantial universality; and the object, as at

[1] Nevertheless, in the libris "Originum seu Etymologiarum" of Isidorus Hispalensis, we find it said (iv. 24): "Stipulatio a stipula,—veteres enim quando sibi aliquid promittebant, stipulam tenentes *frangebant,*" which would seem to be dead against Dr. Heron, who, for the rest, supports his own statement by no authority.

all alienable by self-will, is only an individual external object. Neither the State nor marriage, therefore, are matters of contract. The State, for its part, is very evidently our natural absolute: we can neither enter it nor leave it by will of our own: it is no result consequently of any artificial reciprocal agreement; it is a natural growth, but a growth from reason; it is a realization in time of objective reason, of the rational will. The State is a single national spirit, and it is that spirit which is the substantial contents of every individual subject. These subjects are indebted to it, then, and not it, in the first place, to them. The preservation of the State consequently is infinitely more than the preservation of the individual, and it is the latter's duty to perceive and acknowledge this. As regards marriage, there is a wonderful superiority in the teaching of Hegel to that of Kant. In fact, the sort of good old-maiden Kant is almost even disgusting here, and Hegel has a perfect right to speak of him as having exhibited the subsumption of marriage under the notion of contract "*in its Schändlichkeit*;" that is in its shamefulness, or scandalously. Marriage to Kant, namely, is in so many words, a contracted interchange of the use of the sexual organs, and his whole exposition in connection with it teems with offensive expressions. It is only that old-maidenness of Kant, perhaps, that can supply any excuse for him. He has lived all his life, namely, at such a distance from the kindly mysteries of Hymen, that when he gets a chance in philosophy to approach them he cannot help extending a half-weak, half-wicked hand to the drapery. Hegel exhibits here an admirable contrast to Kant. To him the origin of marriage is ethical. The individual does indeed seek for himself the substantial existence of his own *natural* universal, the *genus*, the family, but the relation of sex in it takes on intellectual quality in a union of love and the spirit of trust. Sentiment, then,—feeling—is still the element in which the family lives, and its rights and duties are moral or ethical rather than legal, for the individual constituents of the family are members of its *one unity*, of its *one personality*, rather than themselves persons, and the legal side is consequently subordinate to the moral. In this way Hegel deduces the necessity of monogamy, and presents the bodily union as rather a result of the ethical one. It is very true that we have all been much interested in certain views in regard to capture in marriage and other facts in its reference of an historical character, but the evolution in time neither dictates the evolution of the notion, nor renders it untrue. So far as time is concerned, religion may have begun in plant-worship, or brute-worship, or star-worship, or whatever worship you please; but, for all that, religion is a principle of reason, and has its own evolution of reason. The evolution in time *generally* is but—if we are to believe Hegel—the evolution of the notion *in representation*, as it were. As such external representation, history, then, is but necessarily a scene of contingency, which contingency gives to the evolution a scattered, partial, miscellaneous look—even a look of caricature; still, nevertheless, the evolution of the notion is but the evolution in time, stripped of its contingency. To arrange law, morals, and politics, according to the notion, therefore, is not really to fall into contradiction with the phenomena of history how motely soever.

Contract, as we have seen, then, is an agreement on the part of two wills—an agreement to a certain performance on the part of each. Now there are certain possibilities in this relation. The one term may have mistaken the other; or expression may not have corresponded to inner intention on the part of either; or performance in the case of the one or the other may fail. Suppose, then, in the first place, a mistake. In this case there is a difference, but neither denies the right of the other: neither denies right as right; each on his own side only insists on *his* right. Nevertheless, there is wrong here somewhere, though both are by supposition innocent in its regard. This, then, is the position of unintentional wrong, unintentional injustice, and the result is simply the civil suit, the action at law. The position is different, however, if we suppose expression in the case of either not to have corresponded with the state of his mind. Here the wrong, then, is no longer unintentional, but intentional; and the result is deception, fraud. But so the wrong is criminal: it amounts to a denial of right as right, at the same time that it acknowledges it in form.

But let us suppose, lastly, that there is intentional and express non-performance of the contract. In that case, the right of the other person is not only denied, but right as right is denied, and we have criminality in terms. *Logically*, as Hegel points out, in the unintentional wrong that gives rise to the civil suit, we have only a simple negative judgment; it is only denied in it that such and such particular is capable of subsumption under the genus, under the general rule; whereas in the case of crime, it is the genus itself, the general rule itself that is denied; and the judgment is of the kind that is called infinite. To say this rose is not red, is to deny a particular, but implicitly to admit a general; whereas to deny that fraud is crime, is to deny the genus itself, is to deny the person to be a person.

This, then, is the sort of external statement of the various positions, but how are they internally? how do they relate themselves to the notion? The notion here is that of will, particular personal will contracting with particular personal will under sanction and prescription of the universal will, of universal right. Now, the fact that it is particular will that is concerned, and in regard as well to a particular externality, some one article of property, introduces contingency, the possibility of accident. Neither will may deny the universal will, and each may insist on its right as particular; but, in its own contingency, one or other may err. Again, in the second instance, or in the case of fraud, universal will is formally maintained by both, but it is secretly denied by one of them. In the third case, lastly, universal right as right is denied, and the individual sets up his own will in its place. Now, it is from this last that the notion of punishment, penalty, evolves itself; and, believing the rest by implication intelligible, it is to this now that we shall confine our attention.

The criminal, then, has done two things: he has negated the universal will, and he has affirmed in place of it his own particular will. How is this disturbance of the true balance to be restored? To negate the universal will is to do something that is in itself null; and this null thing, to restore the affirmative, must be itself nullified. The criminal has resorted to force—a negation, and this negation can only be converted into the affirmative by being itself negated. The negation of the negation, like a double negative, effects position again, affirmation; and punishment is the true remedy. But again, the criminal has set up his own particular will in place of the universal will; and as a free being, he has, in so willing, willed what ought to be, or what ought to be supposed to be, universal. It is but justice, then, that the criminal be subsumed under his own law—force. Nay, as a free being, it is universal will he must acknowledge to be his own true will; therefore, it is but the affirmation of his own true will that he must recognize in the negation of his own false particular will.

The first result, in mere *natural* circumstances, of the assertion of a mere *particular* will as law, is the counter-assertion, and with equal positiveness, so to speak even, with equal right, of the opposite particular—this is revenge. But this counter-assertion, as itself proceeding only from what is private and particular, is itself a new offence, and so there is initiated a progress, or better, a regress *ad infinitum*, as we see in the *vendette* of the Corsicans or of the Arabians. This continuity of an endless repetition is interrupted now by the judge, who, as disinterested representative of Right *qua* Right, rounds the action back into itself through retribution, and restores the universal will—the true will, that is, of the criminal himself. And we can readily see that the judge is the only proper administrator of any such function. His private feelings are not concerned—he is there for the universal only; whereas even the righteous man that would only revenge, that by retaliation would only restore the disturbed balance, acts, and can act, only under private feelings—and probably under *the* private feeling that *his* wrong is wrong *as* wrong, and can only be atoned for by an utter negation—a negation that infinitely transcends the original negation of the criminal himself. The only *legal* compulsion, then, is the *legal* retaliation of the *illegal* compulsion. He who has forced or deforced the law, must be in turn forced or deforced, and that can be realized only where he is seizable, only in his person or property. Of course the word force must be understood to have acquired a width of meaning here beyond its usual physical application: whatever is even *passively* illegal, as a negligence or even a mere omission, is, as infringement of the universal, capable of being regarded as force. In the same way it is allowable to view the sensuousness and mere nature of children as so much force which can be redressed only—raised into the universal of reason—by so much counter-force of training and restraint, discipline and education. The natural will is to the rational will really in the relation of the particular to the universal, and the former must be negated into the latter. To the family as by law established, to the community as by law established, all untutored rude individualism of will or manner may be allowably said to stand as in a relation of force. Even suppose an entire society in a state of nature, that whole society may be convicted of force—force to its own universal, and the resultant *bellum omnium contra omnes* is but the necessary process for the discovery of the heroic will, which, instinctively universal, subjects the rest to itself. Mr. Grote would fain see this war of all against all brought back again; for he would have no standard for the individual but the individual. He is so much surprised, indeed, that any one should think otherwise that he cannot help referring him to what he calls "notorious facts;" and is thus absolutely blind to his own suicidal self-contradiction. Not only are the "notorious facts" he affirms the universal standard he denies; but that he, an individual, and claiming to be amenable only to the individual, should express surprise at an individual, simply for making good his own claim: this is the very *naïveté* of self-deception, the very *naïveté* of self-conviction, and the very *naïveté* of self-confutation. Only in the possibility of such confutation, indeed, is it that there is room for the very existence of the State. Were there no universal, were individualism all, then there were no State. It is the same possibility then, the same fact, that constitutes the very foundation and the origin and the reason of penalty. Many have found much difficulty in this. The Stoics, for example, in assuming only one virtue, necessarily implied also only one punishment, as realized in the laws of Draco, which made death the penalty of offences and crimes alike. Freewill is realized in a necessarily varied externality, however, and the infringements of it are subjected to a correspondent variety both as regards quality and quantity. Analogous variety of punishment, then, is but justice. It is gratifying to observe, however, that there is a decided tendency throughout all civilized communities to mitigate punishments, and all the more gratifying that this does not result from a laxer but from an exacter estimation of law and justice. It is because the *many* so correctly regard the law that we can afford to punish less the *few* who err. In this way, we see that the character and amount of penalty does not depend altogether on the notion, but on the actual historical condition of the particular people. That is the circumstance that explains the apparent paradox: the more a people abhors crime, the less it punishes it. Such a people is secure in itself, and stands not in need of extraordinary examples. It is probably this circumstance that has led some to oppose the punishment of death, and others all punishments whatever. Beccaria, for example, even denies the State any right of capital punishment, and he assigns for reason that it is not to be presumed that the social contract contains the consent of individuals to their own death. But the state is not a contract; and, as the established universal, it possesses a right to claim the sacrifice of the individual for its interests. To others, again, it appears absurd because of *one* evil to will *another*. Accordingly they either reject punishment altogether, or admit it only because of its tendency to intimidate, deter, prevent, &c. Such views, as Hegel points out, however, resemble the lifting of a stick to a dog: they do not really respect man, they do not really respect him as a free being, but treat him as a dangerous animal, that must be kept under. But punishment is an idea on its own account, and has its foundation in the very nature of the will, in the very nature of reason. The true, even to realize itself, must destroy the false: so the false will of the criminal must realize the true universal will, and it lies in the very notion of the relation that the false will should contradict itself, negate itself, and how can that be done but by submitting it to its own law? This is to be borne in mind as against all that moral sublime which encounters us but too frequently in medical books now-a-days. In these we find generally a thousand physiological reasons pleaded in proof that the criminal but obeyed his own necessity, but did what he could not do otherwise; and that the true punishment of the criminal is the rewarding of him by making him, through the infinite cares and privileges of public protection, a mere pampered pet, a sort of humanely and scientifically crammed animal! This is to pervert the very notion of will; this is to pervert the very notion of reason; this is to pervert the very notion of nature herself; for nature, when it is man that approaches her, is herself reason. No; let us to return to health, let us abandon all these pillows and bolsters—all these feather beds of sentimentality on which vice is to fall soft, and let us tell men that they must be men, and that when they declare their self-will the universal will, they must be subsumed under it and abide the consequences. For this there is provided the universal law—for this there is provided the judge, who dispassionately and disinterestedly knows the universal, and dispassionately and disinterestedly can subsume the wrong and the false under it. In the very criminal there lies the universal that is to do him justice. This universal, then, is his own, and in the very fact that it is his own, he has given his consent to its essential and necessary action even against himself. The universal will has a right to negate what would negate *it*, and that very universal will is the criminal's own. The kind of punishment, then, depends on the particular crime, and on the particular condition of society, and that is an affair of *understanding;* but punishment itself depends on the *notion,* depends on reason, and is an inevitable and rational result. "An act of justice cannot be degraded into any mere means: justice is not exercised in order that anything but itself be attained and realized. The fulfilment and self-manifestation of justice is an absolute end, an end unto its own self." It is precisely in punishment that the criminal himself is honoured; and it is precisely by this that such punishment lies in his own act, that he is specially honoured. The particular will that is only the particular will, is an offence to the universal; and must be sublated through its own very self into the universal again, with restoration of the pristine, rational, and absolute unity.

Now, in the relation of crime and penalty, the edge of *internality* appears. The observance of law, namely, may, in many respects, be observance only—an external and mechanical mode of conduct in certain references, without a thought further than the required externality; but this externality becomes *deepened*, becomes reflected inwards, becomes internalized into inner ideal principles of right and wrong, in the relation of crime and its consequences. This is the more apparent when we contrast physical necessity with moral freedom. Only because the sun, the planet, the rock, the river, the sea, the clod, the plant, the animal cannot depart from the prescripts of its universal, is it bound, is it under necessity, and incapable of imputation; whereas it is only because the human being *can* contradict and oppose, and set himself against HIS universal, that he is free and within reach of imputation. It is in the relation of crime and its consequences then, that the majesty of the universal will, which is one's true will, and the nullity of the particular will, which is only one's false will, appear and manifest themselves: and in this way *Right* passes into—*Morality.*

The rights which we have just considered are often named natural rights. There is involved here an essential and fundamental mistake, however. In a state of nature, that is, there are *no* rights—in a state of nature there are only the *unrights* of cunning and of strength. Only in the civil community is it that there are really rights, and these are such as we have just seen sketched in reference to the relations of Property, Contract, and Penalty. The sketch has been slight, but I trust it has not been altogether without true traits. I trust that you understand also, that it has been limited to Right as Right, and that the Moral and Political sections of the book we have had always in view have only been incidentally alluded to.

I have said that for these lectures I had the advantage of the examination of a considerable number of authorities kindly lent me for the purpose; and that the result was to establish my confidence in the exposition of Hegel as regards depth and truth of insight. The consideration now of an objection or two will enable me, by the addition of a word on these authorities, to bring these lectures fittingly to a close.

Röder accuses the Hegelian exposition of "formalism," and of all nations praises the Italian for this that it has "fortunately let the Hegelian goblet pass by." As regards "formalism," there is a certain *outside* show of reason, for the Notion *may* be considered something merely artificial; but as regards the Italians it is Röder who is "unfortunate," for in no part of the world at this moment is Hegelianism more in the ascendant than precisely in Italy: whether at Florence, or at Naples, or even at Rome, under Spaventa, and Mariano, and Vera, it is Hegelianism that, as philosophy, is taught. When Röder further, then, accuses Hegel and his disciples of "obscuring," "degrading," "distorting," "disfiguring," "caricaturing," "the simplest truths of Rights and Politics," "on the rack of an equally clumsy and unintelligible method," by the "trickery" of a new "scholasticism," &c., we have good grounds to suspect him of incorrectness, at the same time that we see *internal* ignorance to be the condition of the *show of truth* that applies to the *outside*. Röder, for the rest, though writing clearly and with much detail, is all too plainly wholly under the power of the biassed and subjective Pantheism of his master Krause. Trendelenburg's is a good book, and by a very able man; but, though, there is latently to be understood disagreement with Hegel, it is the spirit of Hegel that is the valuable element in it. This spirit, too, is what informs the work of Michelet, at the same time that he must be pronounced largely original and valuably so, especially in historical references. What Hildenbrand gives us is a *history* of the notions of Right, and not—at least as yet—a system. As a history, it is most excellent. In all German historical writers on philosophical matters now, there is a single common story, especially in reference to the ancients, but it must be acknowledged that Hildenbrand, for his part, tells this story with perfect elegance and ease, and with the most careful accuracy. I come now to Lassalle, who is a writer at once of original power and great importance. In recent philosophy there are few works of greater mark than his work on Heraclitus the Dark. His work on the Erbrecht also gains more attention daily. But Lassalle is an Hegelian, and he glories in the name. Nevertheless, he has an objection to the *Rechtsphilosophie* of Hegel. This objection I believe to be a mistake, but as it concerns the one pressing question of the day, I shall state it. It concerns, namely, the question of acquired rights, of property, and Lassalle looks upon the ideas of liberalism, of the bourgeoisie, of what we know as the passive political economy of the middle-classes, represented by Mr. Mill, say, as at once narrow and erroneous in regard to it. He surely is not wrong in believing this question to contain the "politico-social thought that underlies our epoch," what "forms the inmost ground of our political and social struggles" now. This it is, he says, that "thrills the world's heart at present;" and "the mere necessity just to refer to this only shows in what soulless platitude and superficiality political principles are understood by the spokesmen of the liberal bourgeoisie." "The isolatedness," he continues, "in which the liberal bourgeoisie places politics—it is that which characterizes its standpoint and its mental horizon, and conditions its performances. It is this isolatedness which gives at the same time to its political diatribes their astonishingly philistine colour," . . . "a dead isolatedness in which the soul has resigned its life and its vision, to lose itself in mere words, and with words, on words, for words, to battle." He would oppose to this word-cultus substantial thought, and he points out the necessity of reconsideration scientifically of many particulars in the science of Right, in order to attain to a scientific theory of acquired rights. He says, "It is now more than forty years since Hegel published his first edition of his Philosophy of Right," and remarks that this work, *from its historical conditions,* could only be a first attempt to exhibit right as a rational organism, and censures his disciples for not having regarded it as a mere logical foundation on which it was theirs to build farther. He regards with Hegel the scientific evolution of will as alone capable of yielding a philosophy of Right; Hegelianism is to him the "quintessence of all Wissenschaftlichkeit," and Hegel's ground-principles, and method will, he believes, always remain. But the principles of Right are, as he also believes, *no stereotyped logical category:* they are substantial ideas that historically change and historically progress. Hegel himself did not, he thinks, sufficiently see this, otherwise he would have treated Law as he treated Religion, and would have demonstrated it in evolution through various historical stages. It is but Hegel himself then that must be used here to correct Hegel. Indeed "Hegel himself and his philosophy bear none of the blame here," is his slightly self-contradictory further avowal; "on every page of his works Hegel is never tired of making it prominent that philosophy is identical with the totality of empiricism, that philosophy stands in greater need of nothing than of penetration into the empirical sciences; reconciliation of *natural* and *positive* right, that was Hegel's object," but his disciples have neglected to carry it out into actual realization in the empirical or historical matter of law. In short, Lassalle would have Positive Law regarded as consisting of but successive historical transformations of natural law, and he proceeds with great eloquence and fulness to illustrate this idea, with special reference to property.

The progress of law, he remarks, is towards limitation of the individual's right to private property—towards the liberation of objects from individual dominion. We see this in the abrogation of *Fidei Commissa* even, though so much is this mistaken, that it is generally regarded as an increase of the liberty of property—a removal of its restrictions. This abrogation, namely, lessens the power of a proprietor over his own property. The same is the case with the "free competition" of the present day. That, too, is vaunted as a giving freedom to the right of property, whereas it is rather a restricting of the power of the private proprietor; for the thought in it is, there shall be no more monopoly, no longer any privileged individuals. The private property, then, that was once possible, is now impossible.

Man, Lassalle substantially continues, at first, like the infant, stretches out his hands to everything—would make all his—recognizes no limits to his self-will. The fetish-worshipper breaks his idol when his desires are crossed, and thus treats his very gods as his property. Long after the rescue of these from such position, man himself continues to constitute to man an article of property. The conqueror regarded the life of the conquered as his; and slavery, at first unconditioned, then conditioned, has only in our own day been abrogated. Formerly one's wife was property, and could be bought and sold. Formerly one's children and one's debtors were so completely in the same category that the former might be put to death by us and the latter taken as slaves. In like manner, the power of disinheritance was but a fuller right of private property, while subsequent legislation has been all in restriction of it. So the slave rises into the serf, the serf from privilege to privilege, into full emancipation. Here even the *jus primæ noctis* is a restriction of property; the seigneur compounds for his right to the very life of the slave by accepting her virginity. The middle ages, though freed from slavery proper, are the very time when the human will can, in all its three moments, be set as private property. Public will is then an object of such property on many grades, and this he illustrates by the privilege of sovereigns and other feudal superiors to arrogate a property in everything, air, and water, and things public, things religious, &c. As for particular will being in similar relations, monopolies, and guilds, &c., are referred to, and as regards individual will in the middle ages, lastly, we are reminded of villenage, and of such rights even over the personally free as the choice by the feudal lord of a husband for his female vassal. The French Revolution Lassalle conceives to have been the sublation of said private property, and in all its three moments. As regards the present, it is incorrect, he says, to call this the age of individualism, and individualism the character of liberalism. Liberalism is particularism (as we may say, classism): it wants freedom, that is, not for the individual, but for the tax-paying, capital-holding particular, and that is a class. This is but a remnant of the middle ages, Lassalle believes, and must disappear. The social question now, he intimates in conclusion, is: whether, in these days, when there is no longer property *immediately* in another human being, such may exist *mediately;* and he proceeds to describe the relative positions of capital and labour as we must daily witness them. It cannot be denied, then, that Lassalle regards the historical progress as *e mancipio*—emancipation, that is, a release from private property; and that such release is equivalent to the positive realization of human liberty. Neither can we well doubt that there is much in what he says highly worthy of our very closest attention (it is curious that we should have here in Edinburgh so recent and striking an example of portion of his doctrine in the changes we have seen effected on the Merchant Schools); still, what concerns us here is mainly the alleged correction of a defect in Hegel. And so far as adhesion to the right of private property is a defect, Hegel must be pronounced guilty of that defect. Hegel undoubtedly signalizes the advantages—the necessity of the institution of private property. Still, it is to be borne in mind, that it is the State that is to Hegel paramount—that to him the State is there with power to sist any contingent unreason of the lower spheres—that the State has a *Machtspruch* over all, and a perfect right of negation. This is manifest in almost every page he writes. Evidently, then, if Hegel is averse to the one extreme, the individualism of such men as Lassalle and Fichte, he is equally averse to the other extreme, the superficial pedantry of those spurious, *passive*, political economists, who believe their laws to be laws of nature, not reason, that need only be allowed to work on like gravitation or a waterfall; and who look forward to that day of light at length, when we shall parson, and doctor, and lawyer ourselves; and when the whole earth will be inhabited only by a single rational community of exchanging animals, with nothing but the buttons of the policeman to clear up, and shine away any foggy nodus of misunderstanding that may arise. That I take to be Hegel's position—a position, then, as it seems to me, that corrects the very correction Lassalle would offer it. It is not correct either to accuse Hegel's *Rechtsphilosophie* of being independent of history, or of dealing only in stereotyped categories, like those of Logic and Nature. The *Rechtsphilosophie* itself contains many references to history, and the whole "Philosophy of History" may be regarded as *just such reference* by itself and at full. Right, besides, is not Religion, as little as Religion is Art: the *Rechtsphilosophie*, and the *Religionsphilosophie*, and the *Aesthetik* must be allowed to prescribe themselves each its own specific character. Neither can it be said, that in Hegel's philosophy of law, Hegel would have all regarded as fixed and stereotyped, a Seyn, and not a Werden, a Being, and not a Becoming. Hegel, on the contrary, is so convinced of the truth of an historical becoming, that he does not regard *Logic* itself as fixed—in the sense, that is, of the impossibility of new categories. He will be found saying, that all revolutions in science, no less than in history, depend on this, that man has changed his categories, and preciser proofs to the same effect might be readily adduced.

It is in place now to refer to Austin, and the remarkable contrast his opinions exhibit to those of Lassalle and Hegel. Of the public good this writer speaks thus:—

"When I speak of the public good, or of the general good, I mean *the aggregate enjoyments* of the single or individual persons who compose that public or general to which my attention is directed. The good of mankind is *the aggregate of the pleasures* which are respectively enjoyed by the individuals who constitute the human race. The good of England is the aggregate of the pleasures which fall to the lot of Englishmen, considered individually or singly." This, you will observe, is the very voice of the modern English spurious *enlightenment.* According to it, what is, is but the various motely individuals, and no *universal* exists, but only a motely aggregate; while *good,* again, is only *enjoyment—pleasure.* These are doctrines that know nothing of morals, nothing of the State, and nothing of the law: these are doctrines that, carried into effect, would, almost in an instant, scatter the race into an incoherent atomism of unconnected and irresponsible single savages. This really is the only word they deserve; yet in his peculiar *Wahn,* so sure is their author of the truth of them, that he says, "When it is stated strictly and nakedly, this truth is so plain and palpable, that the statement is almost laughable." He ought to have said, not almost, but quite laughable, though for a very different reason. This he does not say, however, but continues, this "truism is unknown in that notion of the public good which was current in the ancient republics." "Agreeably to that notion of the public good, the happiness of the individual citizens is sacrificed without scruple, in order that the common weal may wax and prosper; the only substantial interests are the victims of a barren abstraction, of a sounding but empty phrase." The state of Mr. Austin's knowledge, as regards all that constitutes the philosophy of history, is so plain here, that it is useless to point out more than the *dependence* of the individual on that universal—on that common stock which is his *substance,* and apart from which he is little better than the gorilla our so enlightened modern science would make of him. As regards the labouring classes, Mr. Austin speaks thus:—

"It is certainly to be wished, that their reward were greater, and that they were relieved from the incessant drudgery to which they are now condemned. But the condition of the working-people (whether their wages shall be high or low, their labour moderate or extreme), depends upon their own will, and not upon the will of the rich. *In the true principle of population,* detected by the sagacity of Mr. Malthus, they must look for the cause and the remedy of their penury and excessive toil. There they may find the means which would give them comparative affluence; which would give them the degree of leisure necessary to knowledge and refinement; which would raise them to personal dignity and political influence, from grovelling and sordid subjection to the arbitrary rule of the few." The rule of the few is arbitrary and bad, then, to Mr. Austin; but, if only the working-classes would refrain from making children, we should have a heaven on earth! This, with education, is Mr. Austin's panacea. Mr. Austin is, in many respects, a very worthy gentleman; but it is his own wife (an admirable and amiable lady) who tells us, that "the experience of the thirty years which have elapsed since the foregoing lecture was written, does not seem to justify the author's sanguine anticipations." I should like to read you several other extracts here which naively confute the doctrines involved by the wholly innocent but unthinking propos of a disciple who has got by heart only; but I must refrain from want of space. I was prepared also to give some consideration of Mr. Austin's views of Utility, as well as to discuss, at some length, his ideas of the principles of law; but I must now deny myself in these references also. If any gentleman, however, will consider that a command *as such* is to Mr. Austin the essence of law and morals, as well as in *what* he places this command to give it *meaning*, *source*, *reason*, and *authority*, he will be able to form some conception of what I might finally say of him. Mr. Austin, in short, is one of those finical, over-refined, almost female minds, that, without power in themselves, attach themselves blindly to the guidance of another or others; and his book is a work of infinite external verbal distinction, but it has not a vestige of internal thinking rationale. Heron's book is, to my mind, a book much more useful to the *student*, though it is very much of a *pêle mêle*, undigested compilation. Here, too, I have to suppress much. I have now to conclude these lectures by sincerely thanking you for the very kind and generous attention with which you have assisted me in a very dubious and difficult undertaking.

MUIR AND PATERSON, PRINTERS, EDINBURGH.

WHEWELL AND HEGEL

AND

HEGEL AND MR W. R. SMITH:

A VINDICATION

IN A PHYSICO-MATHEMATICAL REGARD.

PREFATORY LETTER

TO

C. MANSFIELD INGLEBY, Esq., M.A., LL.D., Etc., Etc.

My dear Dr Ingleby,—You may remember that I mentioned to you the *first part* of this *vindication*, as designed to connect itself with the centenary of Hegel, now two years ago; and that I requested to be allowed to dedicate it to you. Circumstances interfered with the design of publication at the time; and now that it is accomplished, but in association as you see it, I dare not formally dedicate to you what is allowed, as here, only the second place. Nevertheless, though precluded in this way from the directer action, it is still with this *vindication* that I specially desire to conjoin your name, and I presume, accordingly, to write its preface in a letter to you. Nor will the reason of this special desire of mine be any difficulty to you, for it was you who gently hinted to me the propriety of freeing Hegel, if possible, from the strong prejudice of scientific ignorance to which, since Whewell, he had very generally been submitted in England. I have the hope, then, that you will take kindly my prefatory letter, so far as the paper on Whewell is concerned. I have the same hope, also, as regards the other, its companion, in the mathematical reference; for the occasion of that, too, you know, having done me the honour, I think, to follow its every aspect. I mean, of course, the little newspaper controversy into which I had been already led by the mentioned prejudice against Hegel, even before I had had an opportunity of examining what may be called its root in Whewell. I need say no more to you, then, in introduction, or in indication of the motive of these two papers.

As for the general reader, while I should like him to take

with him the newspaper controversy in allusion (*Edinburgh Courant*, Dec. 21-29, 1868; Dec. 28-30, 1869; Jan. 20-24, 1870), I should also like him to know in what manner that controversy originated.

Sometime after the publication of the *Secret of Hegel*, the newspapers printed an extract, in depreciation of Hegel, from a lecture by a distinguished university professor, on the part of whom, as I both heard and saw, other similar deliverances followed. One of these I at length noticed (*Courant*, Dec. 21, 1868). Hereupon Mr W. R. Smith, then a young gentleman of promise in science, assistant to the distinguished professor in allusion, was induced to communicate with the Royal Society of Edinburgh; and the further newspaper controversy ensued. Mr Smith, in his communications, however, travelled beyond what I considered the original issues, and was, accordingly, not followed by me further than these. But now that completeness in the general reference seems desirable, I attempt to answer his observations in full.

If I am right in this answer, Mr Smith will be found to have fallen only into a mistake, and a series of mistakes, against which I know not that he can claim any set-off, unless on the plea of his youth at the time, the peculiarity, perhaps, of his position then, and the difficulty of Hegel. We might, indeed, be good-natured enough to excuse on these grounds his hasty examination and his unavoidable misintelligence; but justice compels us to think of Hegel, and of the enormous injury that, with the most gratuitous cruelty, has been done his name and his fame in consequence. Thus, very much to Mr Smith is it to be attributed that, in so strictly scientific an organ as *Nature*, and on the part of one of the most distinguished of professors, there appeared (in the number for Nov. 30, 1871) so monstrous a misrepresentation as this,—Hegel "proved that Newton did not understand fluxions, nor even the law of gravitation!" Nay, may it not, in part at least, be attributable to Mr Smith that, with respect to Leibnitz, the same distinguished authority—but no! I respect genius, I respect manliness, I respect Smelfungus, even when he falls foul of the Venus de Medicis, and treats her no better than a cinder-wench!

The *occasions* of these papers, being now, I think, intelligible, I hasten to conclude what I have to premise here. And, perhaps, I had better remark at once that I do not say, as will presently appear, that Hegel has any pretensions to be regarded as a physico-mathematical expert ; but I do say that for his position, and on the whole, he made himself very sufficiently acquainted with whatever he was minded to talk on, and his blunders are surprisingly few and venial. His principle of the *notion* demanded *realisation* everywhere indeed. Physics, mathematics, science in general, therefore, could be no exception. Accordingly, even in these respects, the faithful labour he demonstrates is simply enormous ; and, far from exciting our ridicule, in consequence of the strange look of the new principle in the old matter, it ought to command our sincerest admiration. In physiology, for example, where, from speciality of education, I may be allowed something of the ability to judge, it would be a blunder to attribute to ignorance many queer things that are due only to the Notion ; and as it is in physiology, so it is in physics and mathematics. For myself, again, let me take here the opportunity to say that, as regards these latter, whatever I may claim for Hegel, I disclaim for myself all pretensions to the position even of a student now ; and I beg indeed humbly to apologise for my interference with them. This all the more, too, that I have felt it my duty to stand alone on the present occasion, unsupported by any aid from without. I hope for excuse, however, if not in the compulsion that seems put upon me, then in this, that Hegel, even in the physical and mathematical reference, is only metaphysically, or philosophically, employed. I have hope, too, that, be the result mathematically or physically what it may, perhaps no student of philosophy at this time will regret to have read these papers. It is proper to add, perhaps, that the paper on Whewell was written before the "Lectures" were thought of. And now let me close this prefatory letter by assuring you, my dear Dr Ingleby, that your ideal presence has been a great support to me in the course of it ; and that I am,

Yours very truly,

J. HUTCHISON STIRLING.

EDINBURGH, *October* 7, 1872.

I.

WHEWELL AND HEGEL, OR THE VINDICATION OF THE LATTER IN THE PHYSICAL REFERENCE.

THE writings of Dr Whewell, alluded to in the prefatory letter, consist of those remarks and translations which, constituting Appendix H in the volume entitled by him, "On the Philosophy of Discovery," were communicated to the Cambridge Philosophical Society, so long ago, for the most part, as May 21, 1849.

Into the matter of these writings, it will be necessary to enter with some minuteness, and I begin with the *translations* as constituting the foundation on which *the remarks* rest.

From § 269 of Hegel's *Encyclopædia* (2d Ed. 1827), Dr Whewell's first translation is as follows :—

"Gravitation is the true and determinate conception of material Corporeity, which (Conception) is realised to the Idea (zur Idee). *General* Corporeity is separable essentially into *particular* Bodies, and connects itself with the Element of *Individuality* or subjectivity, as apparent (phenomenal) presence in the *Motion*, which by this means is immediately a system of *several Bodies*.

Universal gravitation must, as to itself, be recognised as a profound thought, although it was principally as apprehended in the sphere of Reflexion that it eminently attracted notice and confidence on account of the quantitative determinations there-with connected, and was supposed to find its confirmation in *Experiments* (Erfahrung) pursued from the Solar System down to the phenomena of Capillary Tubes.—But Gravitation contradicts immediately the Law of Inertia, for in virtue of it (Gravitation), matter tends *out of itself* to the other (matter).—In the *Conception* of *Weight*, there are, as has been shown, involved the two elements—Self-existence, and Continuity, which takes away self-existence. These elements of the Conception, however, experience a fate, as particular forces, corresponding to Attractive and Repulsive Force, and are thereby apprehended in nearer determination, as *Centripetal* and *Centrifugal Force*, which (Forces) like weight, *act upon Bodies*, independent of each other, and are supposed to come in contact accidentally in a third thing, Body. By this means, what there is of profound in the thought of universal weight, is again reduced to nothing; and Conception and Reason cannot make their way into the doctrine of absolute motion, so long as the so highly-prized discoveries of Forces are dominant there. In the conclusion which contains the *Idea* of Weight, namely, [contains this Idea] as the Conception which, in the case of motion, enters into external Reality through the particularity of the Bodies, and at the same time into this [Reality], and into their Ideality and self-regarding Reflexion (Reflexion-in-sich), the rational identity and inseparability of the elements is involved, which at other times are represented as independent. Motion itself, as such, has only its meaning and existence in a system of *several* bodies, and those, such as stand in relation to each other, according to different determinations."

Now, I am a stranger, and I come to this prepared with all that is usually taught and mathematically formulised as regards the phenomena of centripetal and centrifugal forces, of gravitation generally in this universe—what am I to think of it?

What but this? I have before me not an active, sensible, intelligent man, with his wits about him, looking at *the thing* in a business-like manner, and treating it so on the common stage of education and intelligence as it is now, but an out-of-the-way sort of body, a mooning creature with a craze, who, in pure ignorance, non-knowledge, non-education, non-intelligence, simply impregnates a mist of his own with confused figures of his own, that have no earthly application to the business in hand—as a Jacob Böhm or other mere stupid dreamer might do. That any reputable persons of the usual education and position, should be caught with such self-evident, gratuitous, muddle-headed nonsense, fills me with the ordinary surprise, regret, sorrow, which other such spectacles of human aberration,—and they are matters of every day,—are known to bring to everybody. I have no difficulty in the matter. In society I simply avoid, as much as possible, the *bitten.*

This may be allowed fairly to represent the attitude of the unprepared, intelligent, well-educated stranger who first reads the above passage; and it is an attitude, surely, in the first instance, thoroughly well justified. "Which (Conception) is realised to the Idea." How can said stranger possibly realise such a phrase as that to *his* idea? "Connects itself with the Element of *Individuality* or subjectivity," "presence in the *Motion*, which, by this means, is immediately a system of *several Bodies?*" What is all that? he exclaims to himself,—

> "Were such things here, as we do speak about,
> Or have we eaten of the insane root
> That takes the reason prisoner?"

Then "gravitation, as to itself, a profound thought," but "in the sphere of Reflexion," etc. Surely it is but some infatuated wiseacre who can permit himself to canvas for credit by mouthing in that way! "Matter tends *out of itself* to the other." "Self-existence, and Continuity, which takes away self-existence." "Conception, which, in the case of motion, enters into external Reality through the particularity of the Bodies, and, at the same time, into this Reality and into their Ideality and self-regarding Reflexion." What can all that, to the stranger figured, or indeed to any one, seem, but the purest midsummer madness? "It may be sense," will be the thought only of the kindliest reader, "but, meantime, I am simply maddened by trying to think what instantly eludes every attempt to think it." It cannot be wondered at, then, that the conclusion of the stranger is, that he has before him only the pretentious verbiage of an ignorant charlatan.

Let this stranger know now, however, that the writer of the passage translated (or, as we may see, mistranslated), was really a man thoroughly awake—so far as activity, education, intelligence, thought were concerned,—a man so awake that beside even the greatest of his fellows, he would show singularly manifestly, as the man who knew, saw, and could do. Further, let the stranger know the passage he has read is couched (even when well translated) in a language of its own, a language belonging to a peculiar general theory of the universe which, however opposed it may appear to received doctrines of science, really is not so, but is in itself—once seen—perfectly simple, perfectly articulate, and perfectly in accordance with general reason. So prepared, I say, this stranger will probably be ready, and even anxious, to listen further.

Now, it is very difficult to give in any curt formula an intelligible conception of the Hegelian theory. Much depends on an understanding of its genesis, and that is a long matter. Kant and Fichte must be understood for that. Nay, the main ideas of every philosophical thinker, from Thales to Schelling, must be understood for that. Then, prepared as we all are at this moment, so *much* requires to be explained—*for adequacy*—that less than a volume would not suffice. Having, once for all, undertaken to discuss the matter as here with reference to Dr Whewell, however, at least the attempt to explain is necessary, let it be as difficult as it may. I shall leave out a thousand needful considerations then, and endeavour to find such few as will suffice all present purposes.

Hegel regards a thinking being as the ultimate essential *drop* of the vast crass universe. The universe is there for nothing but the production (to say so) of this drop. In the remotest crassitude there is a *nisus* to this drop. Properly looked at, this crassitude will be seen to rise in circles, ever less and less crass, *towards* this drop. This drop, then, is the *purpose* of the universe, and this drop is the *purport* of the universe. It is the principle of the universe, the soul of the universe, the self of the universe. That is—all else being merely ancillary and *for it*—it is the universe. As it is for it that the universe is, its idea is the potential first, or it itself is really the *prius* of the universe. The universe but represents it, the universe is but the realisation, the materialisation of it. It, as an internality, has its own constituent internal forms; of these forms—internal to it—the universe is but the externalisation. Now the very idea of externalisation as externalisation, involves a boundless *extension* of *difference*—a boundless out and out of atoms infinite and infinitely different, presided over by material contingency and material necessity. This, then, is the circumferential crassitude—involved in the very idea of externality as externality; and we may illustrate it by its correspondent idea of internality as internality. Internality as internality, an Ego, is boundless *intussusception*. It has myriads of thoughts, but it itself is a point, and these thoughts are all there in this point, and they are all *through* one another; they mutually penetrate and pervade each other in the single point, which is pregnant with them all. If externality, then, as externality, is an infinite out and out of infinite difference under *ir*rational necessity (physical contingency, etc.), internality as internality is an infinite in and in of infinite identity under *rational* necessity (Freedom, true Free-will). The counterparts are perfectly laid off, the one against the other, and what *is*, the single thing that *is*, *the roc's egg*, is their *antithesis*.

Antithesis must be if there is to be any definiteness, or just anything. Infinite affirmation were nothing; it is something only by returning on itself, only through negation. The universe, then, is, in its *natural* aspect, externalisation, and, as externalisation, the *negation* by which the thinking being makes itself definite, by which it realises itself, for what is externalised can only be its (the thinking being's) own internal spiritual forms. But that being so, it will be possible to trace the spiritual in the material. Explanation of Nature will be the reduction of this to that; as said, it will be the gradual reconduction of external crassitude into the inner reasonable life.

To explain, then, is to reduce into the unity of thought. The farthest crassest nebulæ and hugest volcanic suns must, to be explained, be all resolved into the single essential *drop*.

But the drop itself must have a principle. Now, the drop of the drop is the notion, the act of judgment, the ultimate nerve, the single throb of thought,—the pulse, the rhythm of self-consciousness,—the primeval and eternal syllogism. What is that? It is the schema of universal, particular, and singular. Every concrete is a universal, through a particular, into a singular. This schema is seen perfectly only at last in self-consciousness as self-consciousness; but still, wherever we go, we shall find all but less or more correspondent adumbrations of it. In the very passage before us, this is what Hegel is attempting to show us. In the solar system, gravitation appears as the universal; the various planets, etc., as the particular; and, as a sort of approach to subjectivity, motion as the singular. Dr Whewell did not see that, and he is hardly to be blamed:—how many have?

Aristotle's conception of an Entelechy it is, then, that dominates Hegel. An entelechy is a something that is there on its own account, and realises itself into a whole through assimilation of something other than, different from, itself. Every living thing is an entelechy: it is a principle of life, of something on its own account that realises itself into a whole, a completed system (the particular living being), through assimilation of another, something different from itself. The acorn realises itself into the oak through assimilation of another. The soul realises itself through the body and whatever is offered to the body. An end *realises* ITSELF,—a purpose makes itself end,—

through appropriation of the means. These are *entelechies.* And wherever a principle realises itself into a co-articulated system of members, Hegel sees an entelechy. In his language an entelechy is *Idea*, and the principle that realises itself is *Begriff* (notion). This is the schema of a living, thinking subject. The living, thinking subject has its other (matter, externality as externality, the external material universe) opposite it, and it *realises* itself by appropriation of its other. This is the general principle; and Hegel sees it everywhere in the universe,—sees the universe as nothing but this, as everywhere in entelechies, Ideas, less and less crass, more and more perfect, ascending to this.

This, then, is what Hegel has before him in the passage translated by Dr Whewell, as, I think, will be quite evident when it is re-rendered as follows:—

"*Gravitation* is the true and proper *Notion* (*Begriff*) of material corporeity, *realised* into *Idea* (*Idee.*) *Universal* Corporeity dis-cerns (*urtheilt*) itself, as their underlying general nature and principle, into *particular* bodies, and closes (*syllogises*) itself into the *moment* of *singularity* or subjectivity, as existent manifestation in *motion*, which (motion) is hereby directly (*unmittelbar*—immediately as to sense) a system of *several bodies*."

As intimated, Hegel's meaning, absolutely driven off by the translation of Dr Whewell, will, perhaps, be seen here. This meaning will be *completely* seen, however, only when the equivalents used for the technical words, *Allgemein*, *Besonder*, *Einzeln*, *Begriff*, *Idee*, *realisirt*, *urtheilen*, *schliessen*, *wesentlich*, *Moment*, *Subjectivität*, *erscheinend*, *Daseyn*, and *unmittelbar*, are perfectly understood in the Hegelian sense, for Hegel's dialect is absolutely his own:—

"Universal Gravitation must be recognised as a deep thought in itself, though it is especially by reason of the quantitative applications connected with it, that it has attracted attention and credit, and though its verification has only been placed in *Experience*—ay, from the solar system down to the manifestation of the capillary tube; so that, regarded in the sphere of Reflexion, it has only the import of a result of abstraction generally, and, more concretely, only that of *gravity* in the quantitative consideration of Fall (a falling body), not the import, as given above, of the Idea explicated in its reality. Gravitation directly contradicts the law of Inertia; for, by virtue of the former, matter tends *out of itself* away into another than itself."

This, as a remark on the section (§), is, on the whole, exoteric; but the technical word *Reflexion* would require much too long an explanation to be in place at present. I may point out only that Comte's *Metaphysical* refers, but in *its* way certainly, to the same sphere. Still, the translation will, it may be, prove intelligible on the whole, which that of Dr Whewell hardly is. As a certain support to Hegel's allegation in reference to *Gravity* and *Inertia*, it may be mentioned that Professor Bain (Inductive Logic, p. 13) remarks of inertia, that "it is totally distinct from gravity," and that "it cannot be maintained that these properties are mutually implicated: we can easily suppose matter (considered as inert) without the property of distant mutual attraction, or gravitation; this last property may be fairly viewed as added to or superinduced upon mere inertia; nor can we call the two either cause and effect, or effects of a common cause: our knowledge does not entitle us to make either supposition." Still, I apprehend that inertia and gravitation are but two aspects of the same fact, and that Hegel himself, contradictory as it may seem, would have so declared himself. .

"In the *Notion* of gravitation, as has been shown, there are included the two moments of *Individuality*, and of the *Continuity* that sublates individuality. It has been the fate of these moments of the notion to be regarded as different *Forces*, corresponding to attracting and repelling force, more precisely as *centripetal* and *centrifugal* force, which are supposed, like gravity, to *act on bodies*, and—independently of each other and casually—to tumble together in a third something (a body). In this way, whatever of a deeper meaning lay in the thought of universal gravity, gets extinguished again; and thought and reason will be unable to penetrate into the theory of absolute motion, so long as the so much vaunted discoveries of *Forces* obtain there. In the syllogism which constitutes the *Idea* of gravitation—where gravitation itself namely appears as the Notion which, through the *particularity* of the various bodies, explicates itself into external reality, and at the same time, in their ideality and reflexion into self, in motion, shows itself *shut together with itself* (syllogised),—are contained the rational identity and inseparability of the moments, which in the other way of it are conceived as independent. Motion as such gets sense and existence only in a system of *several* bodies that stand in relation to one another, but in different *determination*. This nearer specification as regards the syllogism of totality, which syllogism is itself a system of three syllogisms, has been given in the notion of objectivity (sect. 198)."

Hegel's sentences are all, as his very individual terms are, syllogisms. He is true to his one single principle everywhere, and his very syntax is the reflecting of a *Particular*, through a *Universal*, into a *Singular*. Each sentence is like a living organism, into which its constituent members are duly folded. Translators of Hegel, then, have a peculiar claim to be only considerately judged; and it would be very unfair to make Dr Whewell an exception. But, leaving Hegelian German as Hegelian German —a dark to Dr Whewell absolutely without a gleam—entirely out of account, must it not be said, that Dr Whewell in the above appears to great disadvantage even as a translator of German simply as German? In the first sentence all meaning is effaced by the words used. In the second sentence again, to leave the words alone, the atrocities that have been perpetrated on the syntax, will be self-evident to every tyro. It is not different with the other sentences, which are all so much "clotted nonsense," whether as representative of the words or syntax of their original. I will only refer to the gratuitous confusion introduced by translating *sonst* "at other times" instead of "in the other way of it," for it applies plainly to the counter explanation by means of mere *reflected abstractions*, dubbed *forces*. Observe "different determinations" in the last sentence too.

The question now is, what has Hegel said in all that? For one thing, he must not be understood to deny gravitation, nor even centripetal and centrifugal forces! Gravitation is to Hegel the very principle and notion of *body*; and of the legitimacy and convenience of attractive and repulsive forces as expedients in calculation, he is well assured. All that he wants to do is to convert all these various materials into the *moments*, and render them into the *rhythm*, of the *Notion*. He would make *Idea* of them, *Entelechy*—an Idea and Entelechy which, however crass and rudimentary, should still show as an analogue of that of *Self-Consciousness*. That is his simple object; to do that is, as Hegel believes, to explain. Throw all into successive entelechies (Ideas), from the infinitely extense circumference to the infinitely intense centre, and to him the universe is explained.

It is not difficult to convince ourselves of the truth of this in the case before us. The section itself is nothing but this *Idea;* and the comments only remark as much. There is Gravitation as the *Begriff*, the unqualified potential *universal* of Corporeity; this appears *particularised* in the *Urtheil* of the various bodies; and these are, as it were, idealised, reflected into themselves in the Motion which is their one expressed actual *Singular*—the *Schluss*. The whole is an *Idea*—a *Notion* with its *realisation*—a realisation into *system* through *moments*. Compared with the Idea of Self-consciousness, *Gravitation* occupies the place of the Logos, Thought; the *Bodies* that of Nature, Matter; and *Motion* that of Spirit, the thinking subject. In regard to an italicised *determination* which occurs above, I may remark that this word (Bestimmung) always refers (when strictly used) to specification according to the notional moments; and it is so that Hegel strikes out the thought of Motion as Motion.

Dr Whewell's translation of § 270 runs now as follows :—

"As to what concerns bodies in which the conception of gravity (weight) is realised free by itself, we say that they have for the determinations of their different nature the elements (momente) of their conception. One [conception of this kind] is the *universal* centre of the abstract reference [of a body] to itself. Opposite to this [conception] stands the immediate, extrinsic, centreless *Individuality* appearing as *Corporeity* similarly independent. Those [Bodies], however, which are particular, which stand in the determination of extrinsic, and at the same time, of intrinsic relation, are centres for themselves, and [also] have a reference to the first as to their essential unity."

One can see from what we may know now, the general drift of Hegelian meaning in this translation, but still too vaguely, too indefinitely, for satisfaction. As more precise, the following will perhaps be also plainer :—

"As regards the bodies in which the notion of gravitation is freely and independently realised, they are determined in their diverse natures by the moments of their notion. One, then, is the *universal* centre of abstract reference to Self [the Sun.] Over against this extreme, there is that of centreless *singularity, immediate,* and absolutely external to its own self, also apparent as independent corporeity [Comets, etc.] The *particular* bodies, lastly, are those which, characterised as well by externality as by internality to their own selves, are centres for themselves, and yet refer themselves to the first-mentioned body, as to their essential unity" [the Planets].

Notwithstanding the general drift of meaning seen in it by light from elsewhere, Dr Whewell's translation, compared with this one, will again appear, perhaps, a mere muddle generally, so far as the exact sense is concerned. In reference, too, to this sense, I remark that the business here (with us, that is) is rather to signalise its true nature than to justify it in itself. In application to Nature, the Hegelian schema often succeeds, but, probably, not always, and perhaps, in general principle, it will never prove wholly satisfactory. Those who already understand what has been said about *Notion* and *Idea* will not require any further comment here.

For the remainder of Dr Whewell's Hegelian translations, I must now refer to Dr Whewell's own work; but, before proceeding to examine his remarks, I think it right to continue my own translation to the extent of his, intercalating such explanatory comments as may appear necessary.

"The *planetary* bodies are, as the directly *concrete* ones, the most perfect in their existence. People usually regard the *sun* as what is most excellent, inasmuch as *understanding* prefers the abstract to the concrete, an example of which is that the fixed stars are in loftier account than the bodies of the solar system. The centreless corporeity, as in its nature mere externality as such, particularises itself in itself into the antithesis of the lunar and the cometary body."

This passage, as rather of an exoteric nature, though still rendered in darkness, is not so badly translated by Dr Whewell. It will probably appear to every one that the association of comets with the moon is an unfortunate conception on the part of Hegel. Still, it must be borne in mind that it is the general position of satellites that, in its relation to the moments of the Notion, dominates the thought of Hegel; and that even while he is so dominated, he has clearly before him all the usual knowledge on the subject as in reference to physical science. I do not seek, at the same time, to induce any one to make credible to himself any such notional copartnership of moons and comets.

"The *Laws* of absolutely free Motion were discovered, as is well known, by Kepler
—a discovery of immortal fame. Kepler *proved* them, too, in the sense that he found
for the empirical data their *general* expression (§ 227). It has since become a current
a phrase that Newton first found the *proofs* of those laws. Seldom has credit more
unjustly passed from a first discoverer to another person. I remark here as follows :—

"1. It is admitted by mathematicians themselves that the Newtonian formulas may
b be deduced from Kepler's laws. The quite direct derivation, however, is simply this :
c In Kepler's third law, the constant quantity is $\frac{A^3}{T^2}$. This being stated as $\frac{A.\ A^2}{T^2}$, and
$\frac{A}{T^2}$ being called with Newton universal gravitation, we get at once Newton's expression for the action of this so-named gravitation in the inverse ratio of the square of the distances.

d 2. Newton's proof of the proposition that a body in subjection to the law of gravitation moves round the central body in an *ellipse*, gives a *conic section* in general, while what is to be proved is precisely this, that the path of such a body is not *a circle or any other conic section*, but the *ellipse alone*. To said proof in itself (Princ. Math. l. I. sect. ii. prop. 1), objections otherwise may be taken ; and analysis has ceased to use it, though
e basis of the Newtonian theory. The conditions which render the path of the body
a certain conic section are in the analytical formula *constant quantities ;* and their determination is referred to an *empirical* circumstance, namely, to a certain position of

the body at a certain time, and the *fortuitous* strength of an *impulse* which it is supposed to have at first received; so that the circumstance which determines the curve to be an ellipse falls outside of the formula that is supposed to be proved, and of any proof of this circumstance there has never been even a thought. *f*

"3. Newton's so-called law of the Force of gravitation has likewise only been inductively demonstrated from experience.

"The only difference to be seen is that what Kelper, in a simple and sublime manner, *g*
enunciated as *Laws* of celestial motion, Newton converted into the *reflexional* form of *force* of gravitation, and of this force as the law of its magnitude is found in Fall. If Newton's form has not only its convenience, but also its necessity for the method of analysis, this is a mere difference of mathematical formula; analysis has long under *h*
stood the derivation from the form of Kepler's laws of Newton's expression and the *i*
propositions connected with it (I refer here to the elegant exposition in *Francœur's Traité élém. de Mécanique*, Liv. ii. ch. 11. n. iv.). In general, the older manner of the so-called proof exhibits a tangled tissue of *lines* of merely geometrical construction, to which a physical sense of *independent forces* is given, and of empty reflexional forms, as the already named *accelerating force*, and the *force of inertia*, but especially the relation of so-called gravitation itself to a centripetal and a centrifugal force," etc.

The numbered paragraphs in the above (as Dr Whewell has it) commencing with "that," reminds that Dr Whewell had, on the whole, before him an edition of the *Encyclopædia* earlier than the last (he names the 2d Ed., 1827, but also "additions" from the "new edition"). My own translations, I may mention, depend on a comparison of Rosenkranz's edition of the *Encyclopædia* with the second edition of Michelet's redaction of the *Philosophy of Nature*. Still, in every edition referred to, the text is essentially the same, and the remarks which I permit myself to make may be held to be unaffected, on the whole, by difference of edition. It is curious to observe how, as a horse pricks up his ears and mends his pace, when he recognises his road as previously known to him, Dr Whewell here makes very good running in his own physical element. Neglecting singulars for plurals and plurals for singulars, the slip of the pen, "fall" for path, sundry unimportant and sundry not so unimportant omissions, his translation of the passage in hand may, on the whole, be named correct.

"The observations made here stand in need of a more detailed discussion than is in place in a compendium. Propositions which do not accord with what is received appear as assertions, and, in contradicting such high authorities, as something still worse, namely as pretensions. I shall not appeal to the fact that, for the rest, an interest in these subjects has occupied me 25 years long. What has been adduced, nevertheless, is not so much propositions as naked facts; and the due reflection is only this, that the distinctions and determinations brought forward by mathematical analysis, and the course it has to follow according to its method, are to be wholly distinguished from those which a physical reality naturally has. The pre-suppositions, the course, and the results, which analysis requires and prescribes, remain quite on the outside of the objections which concern the *physical* value and the *physical* import of said considerations and said course. To this it is, that attention should be directed; what is wanted is a consciousness of the inundation of physical mechanics with an *unspeakable metaphysic* which—contrary to experience and the (philosophical) notion—has alone said mathematical assignments as its source."

The above passage differs little from what corresponds to it in the translation of Dr Whewell. The latter omits, however, the words, "What has been adduced, nevertheless, is not so much propositions as naked facts, and the requisite reflection is only this;" and substitutes for them, "but it is more precisely to the purpose to remark." Vaguer words are sometimes used also than the meaning of the original demands, as "that which is assumed" for "what is received."

k "It is acknowledged that,—besides the basis of *analytical* treatment, the progress of which has, for the rest, rendered superfluous, nay, rejected much that belonged to Newton's essential principles and fame,—what *material* moment Newton added to the scope of Kepler's laws is the principle of *Perturbation;*—a principle, the importance of which is to be mentioned here, inasmuch as it rests upon the proposition that Attraction (so called) is an effect of all the individual portions of bodies as material. There is implied in that, that matter gives itself its own centre. The mass of the particular body is by consequence to be considered as a moment in the *determination of its place,* and the collective bodies of the system determine their own sun. Even the particular bodies, however, according to the relative position which they assume mutually in their general movement, form a momentary relation of gravity *with each other,* and do not merely hold themselves mutually in the mere abstract relation of space, distance, but give themselves, one with the other, a *particular* centre, which, however, in the general system, partly sublates itself again, partly, too, at least when such relation is permanent (in the mutual disturbances of Jupiter and Saturn), remains in subjection thereto."

Dr Whewell's translation here must be pronounced very bad. He seems seldom to see the general idea. Thus the concluding sentence is not only strangely clipped and curtailed, but it is otherwise darkened out of all articulate meaning. The evasion of the difficult "*Inhaltsvolle* Moment" (matter-full, result-full, translated simply "material moment"), is a small matter; but to render "anzuführen" by "accept," instead of "mention," "Masse" by "figure," "sich setzen" by "recognise a reference" instead of "give themselves,"—to use the awkward "as being material,"—to say "their gravity" for "gravity" alone,—and to omit the important word "distance;" these are not small matters. It is important to see here, what Whewell does not, Hegel's striving to find the Notion, Reason, active on these outskirts of existence.

"If now in this way some main features are assigned as to how the leading characteristics of Free Motion cohere *with the Notion,* this cannot be carried out into any fuller details of rational foundation, and must therefore, at present, be left to its fate. The principle concerned is, that the proof of reason in regard to the quantitative characters of free motion can rest alone upon the *notional elements* of space and time, the moments [space and time] whose relation (but not an external one) is Motion. When will science get to acquire a consciousness of the metaphysical categories used by it, and lay the notion of the thing itself, instead of this metaphysic, at the bottom of its reasoning?"

Dr Whewell's respective translation is here again wretched. The important last sentence is wholly omitted, and the first sentence is completely bungled,—in syntax, and every-way. How he could possibly translate "Grundzüge" ("main features") by "features of the path," must remain a psychological enigma. Hegel's honesty too, in regard to the difficulties in the way of his notional assignments, as well as that it is the metaphysic of physics alone that he finds fault with, comes well to the surface.

m "That, *in the first place,* Motion in general is a *self returning one,* lies in the peculiar de-

termination of the bodies of Particularity and Singularity generally (§ 269), to have partly a centre in themselves, and independent existence, and partly, at the same time, to have their centre in another than themselves. These are the notional moments which underlie the conceptions of *centripetal, and centrifugal forces*, but perverted into that n
form, as if each of them existed and acted *independently* by itself, apart from the other, and encountered the other in its actions only *externally*, and consequently contingently. They are, as already pointed out, the lines which must be drawn for the mathematical mode of demonstration, converted into physical realities."

In the greater part of his translation of this passage, Dr Whewell is as unhappy as elsewhere. Omissions as usual occur, and any perception of the original is for the most part absent. "As if they only came in contact in their operations, and consequently *externally*," for example, is a translation quite false and misleading. Here I must point out an error in the text of the usual collective addition, that is corrected by reference to that of the original one (as edited by Rosenkranz.) In the middle sentence, the collective edition prints "zum Grunde liegen, aber darin verkehrt werden;" while in that of Rosenkranz, the same phrase runs,—"zum Grunde liegen aber darein verkehrt werden." There is but a difference of a comma, and of the accusative form "darein," instead of the dative or ablative form "darin;" but the difference is all important. In the one form, the first, we might have felt it natural to translate the last four words simply "but inverse-wise," which would have been wholly to misrepresent, and to miss Hegel's meaning of the moments of the notion having been perverted into the centripetal and centrifugal forces.

"Further, this motion is *uniformly accelerated*, (and, as returning into itself, in turn uniformly *retarded*.) In motion as *free* motion, space and time come, as what they are, as *differents*, to express themselves in the quantitative determination of motion (§ 267 Anm.), and not to relate themselves as in the abstract, or pure uniform velocity. o
In the so-called *explanation* of the uniformly accelerated and retarded motion by means of the *alternate decrease* and *increase* of the centripetal and centrifugal forces, the *confusion* introduced by the assumption of such independent forces, appears at its p
worst. According to this explanation, in the passing of a planet from the aphelion to the perihelion, the centrifugal force is *less* than the centripetal one, whilst in the perihelion itself, the centrifugal force is to be supposed to become immediately again *greater* than the centripetal force; and for the transition from perihelion to aphelion, the forces are in a like manner represented as passing into the opposite relation. It is manifest that such a *sudden turn round* of the attained preponderance of the one force into a succumbing under the other one, is not anything drawn from the nature of the forces. On the contrary, the conclusion ought to be that a preponderance obtained by the one force over the other should not only maintain itself, but proceed to the complete destruction of the other force; and that the motion should pass, either through the preponderance of the centripetal force into rest (by the fall, namely, of the planet into the central body), or through the preponderance of the centrifugal force into a straight line. The only conclusion made, however, is: because, onwards from its q
perihelion, the body moves farther from the sun, the centrifugal force becomes again greater; and because, in the aphelion, it is farthest from the sun, it is there at its maximum. This metaphysical monster of an independent force, centrifugal or centripetal, is a pre-supposition; upon these fictions of the understanding, however, there is no further understanding to be applied—it is not to be asked how either of these forces, being independent, is, *out of its own self*, to make itself, or be made, now less, now greater than the other, and then, again, to destroy, or allow to be destroyed, its own preponderance. Should this, in itself, groundless alternate increase and decrease, be looked at closer, there will be found in the mean distance from the

apsides points in which the forces are *in equilibrio*. Their ensuing transition from this equilibrium is as unmotived as the suddenness of their reversal. It will be easy to discover that, with such a mode of explanation, the mending of a false position by further discussion leads to new and worse difficulties. An analogous confusion occurs in the explanation of the phenomenon that, under the equator, the oscillations of the pendulum are slower. This is ascribed to the greater centrifugal force which is to be supposed to obtain there ; it might quite as well be ascribed to the increased gravity drawing the pendulum more strongly to the perpendicular line of rest."

The above passage is so completely exoteric, that Dr Whewell in his corresponding translation, is in several sentences quite successful. He has found the second sentence about time and space as moments of motion so hopeless, however, that, discovering himself to be sinking in the beginning of it, he has fairly jumped the rest. Then in the middle, after the sentence that ends with "a straight line," the long sentence that occurs in Whewell, we must believe to relate to a different text from either of those before us. The sentence that directly follows is also unhappy. "Just as little without any sufficient reason" (translated above "as unmotived") ought evidently to be *just as much*, etc.

r "As concerns the *form of the path*, the *circle* is only regardable as the path of an *out and out uniform* motion. *Conceivable* (as the word goes) it certainly also is that a uniformly increasing or decreasing motion should take place in a circle. But this conceivability or probability is only an abstract imaginableness [not *think*-ableness], which leaves out of sight the rational quality or qualifiedness [the rationally determined specific nature] alone in question, and is therefore not only superficial but false. The circle is the self-returning line, in which all radii are *equal;* that is to say, it is completely qualified by the radius [to the nature of the radius it owes its own specific nature as a whole] ; there is only *one* specificity [qualifying element] and that the [pervading or] *whole* one. In free motion, on the other hand, where space-quality and time-quality combine into *diversity*, into a mutual qualitative relation, this relation necessarily emerges in the *space-element* itself as a *difference* of it, which accordingly exacts *two* characters. For this reason the form of the path that returns into itself [of bodies, that is, in *free* or absolute motion] is naturally an *ellipse* ; the *first* of Kepler's laws. The abstract distinctive quality that constitutes the circle, manifests itself also in this
s way, that the arc or angle contained between any two radii, is *independent of them*, in their regard a quite empirical quantity. But in motion which the notion has determined [motion as motion, the free, absolute motion in space could only be determined by the notion—reason] it was necessary that the distance from the centre, and the arc described in a certain unit of time, should be comprehended in *one* determinateness, should constitute *one whole* (moments of the notion are not contingently related) ; and thus there is present a space-determination of two dimensions—the *Sector*. The arc is in this way by very nature a function of the Radius Vector, and as in equal times unequal involves the inequality of the radii. That the determination of space by time appears as a determination of two dimensions, as *plane*, connects itself with what has been said above (§ 267) in the case of Fall in reference to the same element, now as
t time in the *root*, and again as space in the *square*. Here, however, the *quadraticity* of space is through the return of the line of motion into itself confined to the Sector. These, plainly, are the general principles on which rests Kepler's *second law* of *equal Sectors in equal times*."

Dr Whewell unaccountably, as it seems, heads this section, § 240. As usual, the translation is infested generally by utter darkness to the Hegelian meaning. Whewell's second last paragraph, perhaps, shows this at plainest. There is much confusion towards the middle of the last paragraph also.

"This law concerns only the relation of the arc to the Radius Vector ; and the time is here abstract unity, in which the various sectors are compared, because it is the determining factor as unity [arithmetically as it were]. But the further relation is that of the time, not as unity [or unit], but as *quantum* generally, as period of revolution,—to the magnitude of the path, or what is the same thing, to that of the distance from the centre. As root and square, we saw time and space related together in Fall, the half-free motion which on one side indeed is determined by the notion, but on the other externally. But in absolute motion, the realm of *free* Measure [Proportion], each element attains its totality. Time as root, is a merely empirical magnitude, and as qualitative only abstract unity. As *moment* of the explicated totality, however, time u
is, at the same time, in its own form definite unity, totality *per se;* it produces itself and *therein* refers *itself to its own self:* as in itself the dimensionless element, it attains in its production only formal identity with itself—*the square.* Space, on the other hand, as the positive *Asunder* (out-of-one-another) attains the dimensions of the Notion v
—the *Cube.* Their realisation, therefore, retains at the same time the original distinction of them. This is Kepler's *third* law, the relation of *the Cubes of the Distances to the Squares of the Times;*—a law that is on this account so very great, because it so simply and directly demonstrates the *reason of the thing.* The formula of Newton, on the contrary, whereby it is transformed into a law for the *force* of gravitation, exhibits the perversion and inversion of *Reflexion* stopped half way."

Dr Whewell's translation here, not so unfortunate on the whole, retains still some of the usual blots. I will only point out that in translating the phrase, "Reich der *freien* Maasze," he has treated it as equivalent to Reich der *freien* Massen ("domain of *free* Measure or Proportion" converted into "domain of *free* masses"). I have written Maasze, though I prefer in general to write Maasse, simply to make prominent the difference of the sibilant letters, as respectively in the short contracted and long open form, in the two German words concerned. Maasze, too, while evidently in the singular, is printed with a double *a*, which, I should think, Masse never is. Dr Whewell now closes with what he heads—"Additions to New Edition, § 269,"—a passage which I translate as follows :—

"The centre has no sense without the circumference, nor the circumference without the centre. This puts to the rout the physical hypotheses which start now with the centre, and now with the particular bodies, sometimes constituting the former and sometimes the latter the original element. . . . . The centrifugal force, as the tendency to fly off in the direction of the tangent, is to be weakly supposed communicated to the heavenly bodies by a fling to one side, a swing, a shove, which they shall have received in the beginning. Such contingency of externally produced motion, as when in a string whirled obliquely a stone tends to fly from the string, has place only in inert matter. We should not speak of forces, then. If we *will* say force, then that w
force is only *One*, the moments of which do not as two forces pull away at different sides. The motion of the heavenly bodies is not any such pull this way or that way: it is the free (absolute) Motion, and they proceed, as the ancients said, like blessed Gods. Corporeity, as in free space, is not such as can possibly have the principle of motion or rest outside of it. Because a stone is inert, and the entire earth consists of stones, that therefore the other heavenly bodies are the same, is a conclusion which sets the qualities of the whole equal to those of the parts. Push, Pressure, Resistance, Friction, Pulling, and the like, apply to another kind of existence on the part of matter than corporeity in free space. Both are matter, indeed, as a good thought and a bad one are both thoughts ; but the bad one is not therefore good, because the good x
one is a thought."

In an exceedingly ordinary passage such as this, Dr Whewell is still unable to achieve perfect success. What he translates are arbitrary fragments too. "Sometimes assign this, sometimes that as the original [cause of motion]." These words in the first sentence do not enable us to be perfectly assured that Dr Whewell understood that by the various theorists, sometimes the sun and sometimes the planets were regarded as the primitive element. Again he says, "If we will speak of Force, there is one Force whose elements do not draw bodies to different sides as if they were two Forces!" It would be difficult to make a more irrelevant meaning of an easier sentence, even if we were specially to try. Probably the whole design in quoting this passage was to bring before the eyes of the reader what appeared the self-evident absurdity about the "blessed gods,"—but that leads to consideration now of Dr Whewell's own special observations on the passages translated, to which I have affixed his own references (*a*, *b*, *c*, etc).

Dr Whewell begins his remarks by apologising for taking any notice of those who, though "the Newtonian doctrine of universal gravitation, as the cause of the motions which take place in the solar system, is so entirely established in our minds, and the fallacy of all the ordinary arguments against it is so clearly understood among us," "yet reject the Newtonian opinions, and deny the validity of the proofs commonly given of them." Now, I can hardly believe that any reader, however much he may be inclined to shake his head at the views of Hegel, will regard Dr Whewell's way of putting it as a fair statement of the attitude, so to speak, of the Hegelian to the Newtonian doctrine. Hegel, though no expert, and not always quite true to the facts, will appear to him, probably, as a man who not only knows but accepts the general arrangements of Newton, and has no desire further but to insinuate into them a theory of his own, which rather absorbs and assimilates than rejects the theory of Newton. There is reason to believe that he will probably think that Hegel is not—certainly *not* as professedly a non-expert—ignorant, but that he is generally well-informed on the Newtonian theory, both as a whole and in its principal details. There can be no doubt indeed that Hegel has taken very considerable pains with the subject, and that though discontented with the *Metaphysics* of Newton, he is not discontented with either his Physics or Mathematics, in themselves and as such. This, I think, very fairly states the general nature of the case. In disposition of his Physics and his Mathematics, Newton has involuntarily recourse to a certain Metaphysic. Hegel, meddling neither with his Mathematics nor his Physics *as such*, would simply replace the Metaphysic of Newton by his own. What this Metaphysic of Hegel is, we must now pretty satisfactorily possess in general idea. It is the Notion. Every act of perception, every act of judgment, every act of reason, is the Singularisation of a Particular through a Universal. Every concrete in existence is a realisation of this, and, as such realisation, an Idea. Every Idea, then, is an explicated Notion, or a Notion *and* its realisation. The Notion itself, even in its own ultimate form, appears as Idea; it is, in that form, the reflexion of a Particular, through a Universal, into a Singular. This is the ultimate pulse of Thought; this is Thought itself; this is Reason; this is the Logos of the Universe. This is the single throb that is the principle of all life, and of all that is. We see this rhythm in its concretest form when we simply say *God created the world.* If God created the world, he did not do so out of the arbitrary self-will of Caliban's Setebos, but out of Reason, out of the necessity of reason, out of his own Freewill. For Will out of the necessity of Reason is Freewill, while Will out of the Self-will (the Caprice) of a Caliban's Setebos is enslaved will, bondage. "*God created the world,*" then, amounts to this:—God reflects the realised universe (a Particular) through his own Logos (a Universal) into Himself (a Singular). Evidently, then, in its own first form, where it is called Notion *par excellence,* the Notion is very fairly Idea. The reciprocal relation of Universal, Particular, and Singular, constitutes a Concrete, an Idea; for even in it there is a Principle which passes into realisation through its Moments. The Singular (take God as such) realises itself through its Moments, the Universal and the Particular. If even this first form, then, which is strictly the Notion, be more than Notion, be Idea, we are driven for an ultimate ultimate to what we have called the Principle of this form, and that was—the Singular. But so-placed, the Singular is Subject, and we cannot think of a subject but as involving a Particular and a Universal; so in the very ultimate ultimate that we would have as bare Principle, bare Notion, we have at once implication of its moments, we have at once Idea. The very ultimate principle of the very ultimate form is the Singular, the Subject, God. In its abstractest form, then, the Notion, and in its concretest, the Absolute Spirit, God, the principle of Hegel coalesces with its own self. To assert, accordingly, that the Notion is the principle of Hegel, is not more true than to assert that it is God—*Geist.* Nevertheless, those who have cried *Geist, Geist,* have in general been blind to what was concerned: Knowing the general schema of Geist, and carrying it vaguely out, they knew not the Notion—*not in itself*—and still less *in its derivation from Kant, if to some extent through Fichte.*

This principle is the Hegelian Metaphysic now, that, not denying, but accepting Newtonian Physics and Mathematics, would simply *replace* Newtonian *Metaphysic.* The principle may be all wrong, but if Hegel believed in it, he is not to be blamed for his action; *and not he, but they only are ignorant—relatively that is—who accuse Hegel of ignorance.*

Before passing on, I would just say one word on the advantages that Hegel's principle, at all events at first sight, seems to possess. It is at once an abstract and a concrete—the last abstraction, the last concretion. It is an ultimate, and, as present, a prime. It is also a recognised principle, a principle *in rerum natura*, and it is a living principle—it is, in fact, the highest principle that all mankind, by necessity of consciousness, have named but never exhibited. It is a unity too, but a unity that in its very nature involves plurality—an absolute identity, but with its own absolute native differences. Universal and Particular are but each the other, and both are the Singular. These are three flexions of the one fact, and each is the other.

The reader must see that we occupy now such a height as will leave little trouble for the demonstration of just one grand mistake on the part of Dr Whewell as regards Hegel; and he will probably also have little hesitation in accepting the distinction between Physics and Mathematics on the one hand, and Metaphysics on the other. Neither will he be unable to forgive Hegel, if, in the desire to introduce this so splendid-seeming new metaphysic of his, he should be betrayed into a little *straining* of the situation now and then. Nay, he will probably find positive oversights in the facts not altogether unvenial in a professed and confessed non-expert, who yet knows so much, and has taken so much trouble to be correct. One thing, however, he will not think excusable even in a Hegel: this latter's unsparing bitterness of tone to him—Newton—whom as a productive thinker mankind have so much reason sincerely to thank and supremely to honour. Even on this head, we can say that *this was Hegel's way*: he saw keenly and he spoke keenly—and he made none an exception, not—nay less than Newton—the good old Kant, whose riches it is that enable Hegel to challenge a place that may yet be the first.

It may strike some here that the "Secret of Hegel," as now explained, being so very simple a matter, it is strange that Hegel himself should have been so silent, or, worse, so very enigmatic about it. How much might have been spared had he been franker, they may think. The thought is not only a natural, but a very just one: Hegel might have made everything easy by a turn of his pen. Why did he not do so? It is to be said at once that the longer he lived, Hegel actually was more and more open in his communications, and that it was probably only his sudden death that prevented a clear, precise, and complete revelation. Human nature is but, at its best, weak; Hegel's halo in Germany before his death was perhaps more truly nameable divine than that of any mortal that ever lived: how can I tell them it? he might have thought. That I have simply taken all the ordinary matter of Metaphysic, Logic, the Philosophy of Nature, Anthropology, Psychology,

Morals, Politics, History, Aesthetics, and Religion—that I have simply taken all this matter and re-arranged it in Entelechies, in Ideas, in Notional Reciprocities of Universal, Particular, and Singular, all mutually inter-connected, all springing from the one single principle that is the principle of this arrangement, and all rounding into the same—how am I to tell them this? Will they see these pictorial inter-dependent reciprocities to be explanation—they who are accustomed to, who expect grounds, reasons?

This is what is meant when I have alluded to artifice at any time in regard to Hegel,—when I have spoken of "the forcible construction of an artificial system on a merely external receipt." It is evident that Hegel,—after all his claims (claims made probably in the first heat of believed discovery)—must have recoiled before literal avowal. Nay, we may be more charitable still,—we may conceive Hegel to have nourished belief in his principle to the last, to have ever fondly dreamed that the "Secret of Hegel" was the secret of the universe, the secret of God, and that it would be found so. If that were so, why should he be at pains to give a psychological history of how he had to come upon it (this secret), of all his experiences, of all his efforts, of all his shifts, in actually setting it to work?

After all, too, is it so certain that Hegel's principle will not prove *the* principle,—the principle of the universe? What is explanation but reduction into thought? And to say things are explained by being *re-duced* to thought, is not that tantamount to saying things are *pro-duced* by thought? What is explanation? Is it not to bring the Particular (all natural existence) through the Universal (all intellectual generalisations) into the Singular (the subject—you and me)? Or may not this process be reversed? May not the Universal (the intellectual subject's own constituent intellectual units) be only realised to the Singular (said subject) through the Particular (actually existent particul*ars*)? The Singular, then, is the Universal,—the latter is the former's necessary constituent Logos—the first is the second, the second is the first—and realisation of the one to the other is only possible through the Particular of actual existence. And what have we been naming all this while—what but the process and rhythm of God? He eternally goes out into His other. Nature, and eternally returns into Himself. God, that is, is Self-Consciousness; for self-consciousness is that which to realise itself goes out into its other, and returns into itself. That is my self-consciousness—that is your self-consciousness. Our life is as Singular to go out into the other, Nature (the Particular), and return thence as Universal (conscious thought) into ourselves. This, then, is the final name for the principle, the "secret," of Hegel—self-consciousness. Self-consciousness, the subject as subject, is to Hegel the Absolute—the one sole, single all-producing root; and the pulse, the throb, the rhythm, the life of self-consciousness is the Notion—the reciprocity of Universal, Particular, and Singular that realises the Idea—that realises the Absolute Spirit.

For the truth of these views, consider the Universe itself—how it is constituted. Would it be a Universe, were it but blank Space and Time? Would it be a Universe, were these filled only with the chaos of a nebula—were these filled only with sidereal bodies, mutually related, wheeling, wheeling ever on mere mathematical reason? Would it be a Universe, even were such sidereal systems inhabited by creatures that went blindly to and fro on mere animal reason—instinct? Can it be a universe till it rushes into meaning, into one, in the thought, the focus, of a Spirit? *It* is *there*, then, only *for* this Spirit—it truly *is* only this Spirit. Thought is the Prius of the Universe,—thought is all that is. All that is, is but a pulse of thought. What is, is God; and God is Self-consciousness. All is His; but as Self-consciousness alone, is it that He *truly* is. Man is the finite Self-consciousness, and he is in the infinite Self-consciousness—in God.

It gives quite another turn to all this, then, to say, that Hegel saw that in actual fact, Self-consciousness was the highest thing in existence, that accordingly he made it the principle of his philosophy, and explained the world to be a continuous chain of attempts to realise the form and rhythm of Self-consciousness up from the most distant circumferential crassitude into the central life of the Absolute Spirit—God. This is to do for the principle of Hegel, what present physical philosophy precisely requires—demonstrate it to *exist*, to be in *rerum natura*, to be a *vera causa*. No one can doubt, that, if we look at what nature everywhere brings it to—nature alone, that is, being regarded as the agent—now to a nebula in blank space, now to inorganic masses in inter-connected whirl, now to minerals of various kinds, now to land, water, and air, now to the dead geological skeleton, now to the plant (from the toad-stool to the oak), and now to the animal (from the tadpole to the elephant), it is self-consciousness that is her highest product. No one can doubt, indeed, that it is only as having produced self-consciousness that nature can be said to have *succeeded*. It is only in self-consciousness that nature first fairly reaches and meets her own self. There at last the chaos of multiplicity is summed, the whole huge many articulated into a shape, which shape is, in its own glance, seized, consumed, burned into a spirit,—the sole true *one*. Well, then, is there not some reason for making this *one* the principle? It is there an actual fact,—the highest actual fact,—and it is evidently the one object to which the many-layered activities of nature in the end tended.

If Aristotle held the man who said *Nous*, to be the only sober man among all the babblers who were bawling out Water, Air, Fire, Earth, &c., I think we are quite justified in holding Hegel,—the man who says Self-consciousness to be sanity itself, beside the representatives of most modern cries. If nature is to be honoured (and explained thereby) for protoplasm and monkeys, much more ought she to be held as honoured and explained in her own highest feat,—self-consciousness. Why, what do all men do when they seek to explain nature? Do they not seek to find notions and a notion in her? What *can*, then, ultimate explanation be but the reduction of Nature to *the notion itself*,—to self-consciousness? That surely is the inmost living principle, and that surely is the single quest of nature,—a quest that, in all her myriad stages, sought on each, fails and falls on all, till it "arrives at last the blessed goal," and leaps up one, the all-intussuscepted one—Spirit—in humanity.

We must not allow ourselves to be blind, then, to this internality, to this empirical truth of the principle of Hegel, even when, for the sake of explanation, we talk of externality and artifice on the part of it and him. So far as that is concerned, we may regard the principle as (from Kant and Fichte) won *externally*, and as then with reference to the ordinary matter of philosophy introduced *externally*. The formal rhythm of self-consciousness in fact is what beats everywhere in the system. As Zeno's stoicism was conveyed by a gesture, so may Hegelianism; for here, too, *pugnus*, and *palma*, and *pugnus* again—that, as symbol, is the whole. In sign, that is the universal, the particular, and the singular. That is identity, difference, and concrete unity. That is notion, judgment, syllogism. That is Logic, Nature, Spirit. That is ponation, sublation, and reponation. That is the myriad-named triplicity in unity that is the systole-diastole, the rhythm of self-consciousness. This rhythm is the origin of the whole, the principle of the whole, the form and matter of the whole. Of this rhythm, as in self-consciousness, the notion is the name and its realisation is idea. Or call this realisation entelechy—the one single realised self-end, self-object, that is—then notion is the subjective side of this entelechy, idea the objective one. The rhythm, as self-realising, is notion; as self-realised, idea. The ultimate nerve of self-consciousness is universal, particular, and singular; that, too, is the ultimate expression of the notion; and that finally, as implying realisation of the particular through the universal in the singular, is the ultimate form of the idea.

I think I may take it for granted now, then, that the reader has it quite plainly before him how much Dr Whewell was speaking beside the point when he referred to Hegel as rejecting the Newtonian hypothesis, and denying the validity of its proofs. Hegel accepts Newton's physical fact of universal gravitation, and mathematically denies not his proofs: metaphysically only he would name and explain otherwise. In the same way when he praises the physical theories of Aristotle, as compared with certain modern empirical theories, we are not to accuse him of ignorance in regard to the latter, because he finds the metaphysic they bring with them poor. In this connection, he says, for example, "the conception that the heavenly bodies would continue to move in a straight line, unless *fortuitously* attracted by the sun is an empty thought;" but this by no means argues ignorance of physics, though he certainly prefers to consider the solar system eternal and necessary, in virtue of his metaphysics. "This is nothing else than that Epicurus judged according to *analogy*, or made what is called *explanation* the principle of the analysis of nature; and this is the principle that still obtains in the usual natural science. We make experiments, observations, which concern sensations easily surveyed. We come thus to general ideas, laws, forces, etc., as Electricity, Magnetism; and we then apply these to such objects and actions as we cannot ourselves directly experience . . . Thus the nerves are pictured to consist of quite minute spheres, invisible even under the most powerful lenses, the last of which spheres it is, however, that, on occasion of a touch, leaps off and hits the soul." This, again, if a mockery of metaphysic is not by any means to be understood as ignorance of what relates to electricity, magnetism, and physiology.

These remarks, I take it, exhaust Dr Whewell's whole case against Hegel, but it may be desirable to see as much in the details as well.

To assist the particular application now in place, I make the following extracts from Dr Whewell's own statements in his History of the Inductive Sciences, Chapters iv. (Book v.), to ii. (Book vii):—

"The leading thought which suggested and animated all Kepler's attempts was true, and, we may add, sagacious and philosophical; namely, that there must be *some* numerical or geometrical relations among the times, distances, and velocities of the revolving bodies of the solar system.

"Many of Kepler's guesses . . . have been confirmed by succeeding discoveries in a manner which makes them appear marvellously sagacious; as, for instance, his assertion of the rotation of the sun on his axis, before the invention of the telescope, and his opinion that the obliquity of the ecliptic was decreasing, but would, after a long-continued diminution, stop, and then increase again.

"Kepler's talents were a kindly and fertile soil, which he cultivated with abundant toil and vigour; but with great scantiness of agricultural skill and implements. Weeds and the grain throve and flourished side by side almost undistinguished; and he gave a peculiar appearance to his harvest, by gathering and preserving the one class of plants with as much care and diligence as the other.

"This rule" (Kepler's third law) "is expressed in mathematical terms by saying that the squares of the periodic times are in the same proportion as the cubes of the distances; and was of great importance to Newton in leading him to the law of the sun's attractive force.

"Kepler always sought his *formal* laws by means of *physical* reasonings.

"Kepler replunges himself in the relations of music to the motions, the distance, and the eccentricities of the planets. . . . But . . . recollect that Newton has sought for analogies between the spaces occupied by the prismatic colours and the notes of the gamut.

"The law, as a *formal* rule, was complete in itself.

"The physical theories of Kepler, and the reasonings of other defenders of the Copernican theory, led inevitably, after some vagueness and perplexity, to a sound science of mechanics.

"We make a transition from the *formal* to the *physical* sciences,—from time and space to force and matter,—from *phenomena* to *causes*.

"*Natural* motion is stronger towards the end, as the motion of a falling body.

"Kepler's doctrine is that a certain force or virtue resides in the sun, by which all bodies within his influence are carried round him . . . comparing it . . . to the Magnetic Power, which it resembles in the circumstances of operating at a distance, and also in exercising a feebler influence as the distance becomes greater.

> 'What if the sun
> Be centre to the world ; and other stars,
> By his attractive virtue, and their own
> Incited, dance about him various rounds?'—*Par. Lost*, B. viii.

"It was undoubtedly a great advance towards the true theory of the universe to consider the motion of the planets round the sun as a mechanical question, to be solved by a reference to the laws of motion, and by the use of mathematics. So far the English philosophers appear to have gone before the time of Newton. Hooke, indeed, when the doctrine of gravitation was published, asserted that he had discovered it previously to Newton. . . . In 1674 . . . he (Hooke) distinctly states that the planets would move in straight lines; if they were not deflected by central forces.

"The proposition that the attractive force of the sun varies inversely as the square of the distance from the centre, had already been divined, if not fully established. . . These inferences were all connected with Kepler's law.

"Newton had so far been anticipated, that several persons had discovered it to be true, or nearly true ; that is, they had discovered that if the orbits of the planets were circles, the proportions of the central force to the inverse square of the distance would follow from Kepler's third law.

"The two steps requisite for the discovery [of the sun's force on the different planets] were to propose the motions of the planets as simply a mechanical problem, and to apply mathematical reasoning so as to solve this problem, with reference to Kepler's third law considered as a fact.

"The inference of the law of the force from Kepler's two laws concerning the elliptical motion was a problem quite different from the preceding, and much more difficult.

"He [Newton] has traced its consequences [those of the proposition relating to force in different points of an orbit], and solved various problems flowing from it with his usual fertility and beauty of mathematical resource ; and has there shown the necessary connection of Kepler's third law with his first and second.

"We have already seen that, by calculating from Kepler's laws, and supposing the orbits to be circles, the rule of the force appears to be the inverse duplicate proportion of the distance ; and this, which had been current as a conjecture among the previous generation of mathematicians, Newton had already proved by indisputable reasonings.

"Kepler's laws were merely *formal* rules governing the celestial motions according to the relations of space, time, and number ; Newton's was a *causal* law.

"As Newton's laws assumed Kepler's, Kepler's laws assumed as facts the results of the planetary theory of Ptolemy.

"Those which he [Newton] had more peculiarly to take hold of, were the facts of the planetary motions as given by Kepler, and those of the moon's motions as given by Tycho Brahe and Jeremy Horrox."

From these extracts it will appear that Newton's merit was to complete, chiefly through unrivalled mathematical powers, the theory of gravitation—out of various materials already in great part provided to his hands, and that among these materials by far the most important were those which bore to be discoveries of Kepler. Nay, it will even appear that the main proposition, at all connected with gravitation, was not only deducible, but actually had been deduced, from Kepler's laws, especially the third. Now, Hegel says no more than this, and he only objects to the vulgar transference of the glory of *discovery* to the allegation of *proof*. *Apply* these laws, as you may, says Hegel, no mathematical process can supersede the *discovery* of them; and the allegation of their *proof*, which just means their further application and connection, ought not to be allowed to interfere with the merit of the discoverer. That Hegel preferred Kepler to Newton (if he really did so), I should consider almost a solitary instance of departure on his part from his own admirably self-consistent sound sense. Newton was undoubtedly by much the greatest physico-mathematical thinker that ever lived, and, compared with even the genial Kepler, probably an incommensurably deeper nature.*

Still it is difficult to understand the wrath of Whewell† and others, at this simple statement of Hegel:—

> "Kepler discovered the laws of free motion; a discovery of immortal glory. It has since been the fashion to say that Newton first found out the proof of these rules. It has seldom happened that the glory of the first discoverer has been more unjustly transferred to another person."

It is in a perfect white rage that Whewell remarks here:—"It may appear strange that any one in the present day should hold such language." But I for one would beg to be allowed to ask why? I do not take one jot or tittle from the fame of Newton, who worked up Kepler's laws and other materials into wonderful connection—into the connection of the single theory which is the glory of the human intellect; but why should I not be allowed to point out that no mathematical operation is adequate to discovery of a wholly new qualitative fact, which merit, in the case of his laws, belongs to Kepler? To say that the *proof* was not alleged as in supersession of the *discovery*, is not to convict Hegel of ignorance. For the transference of the glory from the *discoverer* to the *prover* was a wide-spread vulgar prejudice, to which it was perfectly in place for Hegel to object. I think we may say as much as this even though the merit of the application on the part of Newton were infinitely greater than that of discovery on the part of Kepler. It is in vain to

* It is thus eloquently that Whewell himself speaks of Newton:—

"The ponderous instrument of synthesis, so effective in his hands, has never since been grasped by one who could use it for such purposes; and we gaze at it with admiring curiosity as on some gigantic implement of war, which stands idle among the memorials of ancient days, and makes us wonder what manner of man he was who could wield as a weapon what we can hardly lift as a burden."

It is this enormous mathematical power that *is* Newton; the ideas it wrought up were, according to Whewell, for the most part already to hand. Kepler himself shall have known "that gravity was the common quality of bodies, that the attraction of the moon was the cause of the tides, and that the irregularities of the lunar motion were due to the conjunct action of sun and earth."

† See *History of the Inductive Sciences*, vol. ii., p. 188.

point to Newton's independent labours as regards the moon in objection here. It must be admitted at last that the theory of gravitation is more indebted to Kepler's laws than Kepler's laws to the theory of gravitation. The latter certainly gave connection, meaning, completion to the former; but the important fact is that Kepler's laws were first, and that the theory of gravitation lay in them. It is really difficult to understand the offence taken at Hegel's vindication of the glory of Kepler's laws for the *discoverer* from the *prover*, or the assumption of that vindication as a denial of gravitation, and a direct attack on Newton.

Hegel's facts are precisely Whewell's facts. It is Whewell who asserts Kepler's third law to have been "of great importance to Newton in leading him to the law of the sun's attractive force"; and Hegel asserts no more. Again, it is Whewell points out the distinction between *formal* and *physical, phenomena* and *causes, formal relations of space and time, and a causal law;* and Hegel means precisely the same thing when he grumbles about the "*reflexion*" of Kepler's rationalised phenomena into Newton's abstraction of causal force. "Kepler's laws," says Dr Whewell, "were merely formal rules governing the celestial motions according to the relations of space, time, and number; Newton's was a *causal* law:" and this is accurately what Hegel said.

But let us pass now to Dr Whewell's particular remarks, for the discussion of which we are at last, perhaps, fully prepared.

Not pretending "to offer here any opinion upon the value and character of Hegel's philosophy," Dr Whewell still intimates that examination of the other parts of the Hegelian system would confirm the very unfavourable judgment he finds himself compelled to pronounce; but it is not difficult to pardon a solid man even when he blunders by precipitation, and this I pass.

Expressing surprise, though only with the most Jovine twitch of the eyebrow, that Hegel should offer *his* proof (he only offers his metaphysic) of Kepler's laws, Dr Whewell proceeds to what, marked (*a*), concerns these laws in Newton's reference. He states Hegel's averment (*b*) to be, "it is allowed by mathematicians that the Newtonian formula may be derived from the Keplerian laws." Dr Whewell evidently takes great offence at the word formula; "but let us see," he says, "what he" (Hegel) "says further of this derivation of the Newtonian 'formula' from the Keplerian law. It is evident that by calling it a *formula*, he means to imply, what he also asserts, that it is no new law, but only a new form (and a bad one) of a previously known truth." Now, I think we may say at once, that Hegel never meant to *imply* any such thing, and, consequently, that he does not *assert* it. Hegel pays, in his own way, his tribute of admiration to the thought of gravitation, and

—*adopts* it. He only points out that, for the phenomena, it is what he calls a form of *reflexion*. Dr Whewell admits "I am not able to assign any precise meaning to the *reflexion*, which is here used as a term of condemnation, applicable especially to the Newtonian doctrine;" he accordingly entirely puts himself out of court as regards the application of this term; and we can say at once that, springing from a certain point of view, it certainly does not carry with it the *special* condemnation of Newton which Whewell attributes to it. To understand the meaning of the term *reflexion* (certainly a prerequisite for a judge that would say anything to the purpose) would demand an understanding of a whole volume—of that volume of the Logic, namely, which Hegel superscribes "*Wesen*." That volume concerns what Hegel calls "previous metaphysic," and endeavours to show, so far as *reflexion* is concerned, that there was a tendency at a certain historical epoch to *reflect* phenomena into what were called general principles, but which remained, nevertheless, mere general *names*. Certain phenomena are called *manifestations*, for example, and are reflected into a supposed unit that is to stand for them, named *force*. Hegel acknowledges this to be historically a necessary stage of generalisation, but he denies it to be the final one. These abstract *forces* he would replace in all cases by the *notion*. Gravitation, then, however true on that stage, is but a form of reflexion. Hegel, however, would never assert that his supposed metaphysical improvement was meant to show that Newton's theory of gravitation, with all its mathematical consequences, was technically *incorrect*. Far from it. He has no eye whatever in that direction. He is merely busied on *metaphysical* explanation, and accepts physical facts and mathematical demonstrations towards it. Dr Whewell misses all this, and only sees in Hegel's statements—what does not exist there, and never was intended to exist there—charges of *technical incorrectness* against Newton. It may appear small, then, but it really has some bearing here to point out that Hegel does *not* throw this ugly reproach of *formula*, as Whewell thinks it, at Newton's head. Hegel does not speak of Newton's formula, but of Newton's formula*s*, and he means no reproach by the term. Dr Whewell ought to have known this: there are present not only a plural noun, adjective, and article, but even a plural verb.

There is no reason whatever for asserting, as Dr Whewell does, that Hegel infers the Newtonian law not to be "an additional truth." It cannot be said even that Hegel denies to Newton "the discovery of the cause which produces a certain phenomenal law." So far as the operation of *reflexion* is concerned, Hegel admits that. He only grumbles that the intervention of the *reflexion* was not in the case of Kepler's laws an assistance to the *notion*.

Dr Whewell proceeds :—

"'The Newtonian formula may be derived from the Keplerian law.' It was professedly so derived; but derived by introducing the Idea of *Force*, which Idea and its consequences were not introduced and developed till after Kepler's time."

Precisely what I say, says Hegel, only that I remark of the *reflexion—force*, things that you do not understand.

"'The Newtonian formula may be derived from the Keplerian law.' And the Keplerian law, may be derived, and was derived, from the observations of the Greek astronomers and their successors ; but was not the less a new and great discovery on that account."

Hegel here would have his own reflections about what the *thought* of Kepler *put into* the observations of the Greek astronomers, and into those of others after them ; but he would be disposed to remark, well, in a certain way, agreed, but what is that to anything I have said? Kepler gave the law, Newton the *force* of gravitation as the *cause*, and I grumble that the latter did not proceed to what I call the *notion of reason !*

Under (*c*) Hegel remarks that the $\frac{A^3}{T^2}$ of Kepler's law being stated as $\frac{A.\ A^2}{T^2}$, and $\frac{A}{T^2}$ being named with Newton universal gravitation, we get at once Newton's expression for the law concerned. Dr Whewell's correspondent remark, representing Hegel to say, Newton "*calls*" $\frac{A}{T^2}$ universal gravitation, and that he "defines" gravitation to be $\frac{A}{T^2}$, whereas Newton only "*proves* that in circles the *central force* (not the *universal gravitation*) is as $\frac{A}{T^2}$," is incorrect to the import of Hegel's words, and in every way small.

Dr Whewell next takes up Hegel's statement (*i*), which is this:—

"Analysis has long understood the derivation from the form of Kepler's laws of Newton's expression and the propositions connected with it (I refer to the elegant exposition in Francœur, &c.). In general, the older manner of the so-called proof exhibits a tangled tissue of *lines* of merely geometrical construction to which a physical sense of *independent forces* is given, and of empty reflexional forms as the already-named *accelerating force*, and the *force of inertia*, but especially the relation of so-called gravity itself to a centripetal and a centrifugal force, etc."

Now, really, Hegel has nothing at heart but his metaphysic here: he has not the slightest idea of calling the physics or the mathematics as such bad, but only the metaphysic they involve. He admits that "Newton's form has not only its convenience, but also its necessity for the method of analysis;" but he observes, "this is a mere difference of mathematical formula," meaning thereby that the *reason* which he sees in the celestial motions is untouched by the mathematical processes, let them be what they may. It is only in reference to the single rational notion present in the phenomena that he demurs to the splitting up of that unity for mere mathematical purposes into lines this way for centripetal forces, and lines that way for centrifugal forces. Such fictions lie not in the notion, he intimates, and are mere conveniences for the mathematical operations which, in their own way, are certainly correct.

It is hardly worth while following Dr Whewell more closely on this point; he wholly misapprehends the import of Hegel's relative speech, and says a variety of things quite beside the question. He holds, for instance, that Hegel wants "to show that the 'lines' of the Newtonian construction are superfluous." That is simply absurd; Hegel expressly grants the necessity of such construction according to a certain method mathematically, and would only point out the interference of these lines with his own notion metaphysically. What follows on Whewell's part, about analysis and geometry, is, in ignorance of Hegel's object, similarly speech in the air; and when he says, "so much for Newton's comparison of the forces in different circular orbits, and for Hegel's power of understanding and criticising it," we would only remark, so much for Dr Whewell's power of understanding and criticising Hegel.

We have much the same thing to see in Dr Whewell's remarks under (*o*). Here he objects to Hegel talking of "the velocity in an elliptical orbit alternately increasing and diminishing" in connection with centrifugal and centripetal forces. He asserts Newton nowhere to employ "centrifugal force" in his explanations, but acknowledges that reference to that force "is introduced in some treatises, and may, undoubtedly, be used with perfect truth and propriety." That is quite enough to justify Hegel in demonstrating the *metaphysical* incongruities in all such explanations; and Dr Whewell's remarks here are not only uncalled for, but vexatious. He cavils at Hegel's use of the words *uniform motion*,—words understood in all their senses quite as well by Hegel as by Whewell; and he misplaces in his quotation (*p*) *centrifugal* and *centripetal*, which, however, are not securely placed by Hegel himself. His own statement is a complete proof of the confusion which the hypothesis of centripetal and centrifugal forces introduces into the *metaphhysical* notion, let them end in what mathematical correctness they may. Hegel, then, is really untouched when Whewell concludes here thus:—

"This reasoning is so elementary, that when a person who cannot see this, writes on the subject with an air of authority, I do not see what can be done but to point out the oversight, and leave it."

Dr Whewell goes on to animadvert (*q*) on Hegel's reference to *another* mode of explanation in this matter, and triumphantly exclaims that this *other* mode is the same as the former one. I can see no justification for this in Hegel's text: so far as I see, Hegel refers there to no more than one mode of explanation.

I know not, then, that Hegel can be confuted of any technical error here; even when he ignores the mechanical explanation of acceleration and retardation which Dr Whewell himself details to us very clearly. Hegel, in that, has still only the one object: the metaphysical confusion introduced by the only *convenient* reflexional forms of two opposed forces. And Dr Whewell, though he there certainly says something to the point, does not altogether remove this metaphysical confusion when he remarks that, though there is supposition of two forces, —one intrinsic, and one extrinsic,—there is no supposition of "two distinct forces both extrinsic to the motion."

Dr Whewell's reference (*n*) falls into this remark, in regard to the subject of which we may allowably say in general that, while Hegel plays his metaphysics too close upon physics quite to come off scatheless, his opponent, even on his own side, is too fastidious to be quite secure. We have all heard too much of centrifugal and centripetal forces to be as fierce against Hegel in this matter as Whewell is. In the Ninth Edition (1844) of "Conversations-Lexicon," under the heading Gravitation, we can still read a doctrine of the two forces not dissimilar from that on which Hegel comments. There we learn that if no other force than gravitation acted on the planets, they would tend in a straight line towards the sun; and that, therefore, we must assume another force, which shall have bestowed in the beginning of its movement a push sidewards on each planet. It is to the two forces that the curve of movement is due, which curve Newton proved to be necessarily a conic section, whether parabola, hyperbola, or ellipse, depending upon the magnitude of the tangential or centrifugal force. Nor are our own English encyclopædias and elementary works discrepant.*

The next point that Dr Whewell notices is (*d*) Hegel's objection that for the path of the planets Newton's proof gives a *conic section* in general, and not an *ellipse* in particular. And here Dr Whewell intimates that an ellipse is no necessity of the

* Professor Bain of Aberdeen (*The Senses and the Intellect*, 2d ed., p. 521), has the following:—

"Newton had for years been studying the celestial motions: by the application of the doctrines of the composition and the resolution of forces to the planetary movements, he had found that there were two actions at work in the case of each planet; that one of these actions was in the direction of the sun, and the other in the direction of the planet's movement at each instant—that the effect of the first, acting alone, would be to draw the body to the sun, and the effect of the second, acting alone, would be to make it fly off at a tangent, or in a straight line through space."

Whewell abuses Hegel for saying this in 1830, and here Professor Bain, who, *bekanntlich*, might fill any physical chair in the kingdom, says the same thing in 1864!

nature of the case: planets might move in circles, and some planets actually do move "in orbits hardly distinguishable from circles." Hegel's idea certainly is that the ellipse is a necessary outcome of *the notion* on this the stage of free motion according to the relations of time and space as moments. If planets do move in circles, or even if planets might move in circles, Hegel would have here to confess a failure. It would be his metaphysic that in that event would suffer, however, rather than his knowledge of physics. In the meantime, the fact is that the curve of movement still remains an ellipse, and Hegel so far is not in error.

Dr Whewell now objects (*e*) to Hegel's critique of the "push sidewards," which has been mentioned as the necessary assumption in explanation of the check to gravitation that results in the curve of movement. But here Hegel, his own point of view being considered, is perfectly unassailable. What Hegel seeks is the necessary demonstration of reason. If, then, to the theory of the particular ellipse, it is necessary only to suppose that the planet was in such and such an empirical position, and that then such and such a push or kick was administered to it to launch it on its way, such a man as Hegel has no alternative but to say, You tell me stories for children; I want proof; even in your alleged proof the most important condition is unproved and remains a mere assumption: what is all this you prattle —about times infinitely far back, and accidental positions then, followed by pushes we know not from what or how? Dr Whewell, then, is here seen to be again speaking quite into the air. We know nothing about "why" he keeps on saying angrily and loudly. Pooh! says Hegel, that is all I'm talking about: you don't suppose I am criticising your theories from your own grounds, mathematical and physical, do you? In short, Hegel's whole stand-point, quite unknown to Whewell and others, will be clear from this extract from the *Logik* (vol. i., p. 416):—

"It is a great service to enable us to know the empirical numbers of nature, as the distances of the planets from each other; but it is an infinitely greater service, causing the empirical quanta to disappear, to raise them into the *universal form* of quantitative relations, so that they become moments of a law; immortal services which Galilei for the principle of Fall, and Kepler for the movement of the heavenly bodies, have achieved. The laws thus found they have *proved* in this sense, that they have shown the whole compass of the particulars of observation to correspond to them. But yet a still higher *proof* is required for these laws; nothing else, that is, than that their quantitative relations be known from the qualities or special notions, as time and space, that are correlated."

This will enable us to see something of the wants of Hegel, and to understand why he took so much offence at the "current phrase" about Newton having found the *proofs* for Kepler's laws. According to Hegel's meaning of the words, Kepler had *proved* his laws, so far as they could be proved without intervention of *philosophy proper*, and it was unjust to say that for proof these laws had to wait for Newton, whose merit it was only mathematically to clear and connect them—them and the principle of gravitation that lay in them. *Proof* means to Hegel reduction to the notion of reason; and that is what ought always to be borne in mind in his regard, or that what Hegel means by proof is Hegel's own metaphysic.

Dr Whewell now remarks that "Hegel himself has offered proof of Kepler's laws," and to this he turns himself with some curiosity, but with what result it is easy to surmise. Dr Whewell, that is, merely finds himself in a region unintelligible to him, and to him also necessarily unreasonable and absurd. The point he first signalises here is (*r*) what concerns the ellipse as the necessary curve of motion. All that Hegel says in that reference amounts to this:—The circle being determined by the radius has but one quality, perfect uniformity; but the relations of space and time involve *difference*, and that difference asserts itself in the free motion that results from these relations: its curve of movement is the double-centred ellipse. I do not ask any uninitiated reader not to laugh here; but I will ask him to consider that Hegel is engaged rationalising the origin of things. Why there is such a thing as space, and such a thing as time, and according to Hegel's meaning of *why*—really, so far, Hegel succeeds very well. From these he proceeds, as we see, to find motion and matter implied in the very relations of time and space—nay, implied in the same relations, the very nature of the path of motion. In this I do not say he succeeds, but I certainly say the enterprise is a thoroughly legitimate one, and that the outcome of it, even so far, is at least neither despicable nor ridiculous. At all events, it is not as Whewell and others suppose it,—the mere conceited ravings of ignorant and wholly incompetent bias. There is still here at work the most alert, the most thoroughly-prepared, the most practical, the most irresistible intellect that I, for my part, know. What Whewell makes of it is simply nonsense; his translation contains not a dream of what is meant by the *difference* (he says differences) that is held to emerge naturally from the very relations of space and time. Whewell, too, evidently looks at it all as a physico-mathematician, in which aspect it can have no meaning; for it can have no reference to physico-mathematical science as such, but simply to metaphysic. That those who are physicists, then, and nothing more, should express disgust at such utterances of Hegel, and should pronounce it a loss of time to hear more of them, cannot prove surprising to any one who will simply look at the state of the case.

Dr Whewell here objects also (*m*) that the "line returning into itself," which Hegel supposes himself to prove for free motion does not, in consequence of "movable apses," always in point of fact exist. The objection is a small one, however, and can hardly be acknowledged to apply, especially in view of the admission of *Perturbations* on the part of Hegel. At the same time, it is to be pointed out, that Dr Whewell owns himself unable to find "precise meaning" in Hegel's respective deliverance.

Under (*s*), which concerns Kepler's second law ("that the elliptical sectors swept by the radius vector are proportional to the time"), we may allow Dr Whewell's objection simply to stand in its own shape: "If we could regard this as reasoning, it would not prove the conclusion, but only, that the arc is *some function or other* of the radii." By the word "*prove*," Dr Whewell has in his eye not the notion, but some mathematical process.

Dr Whewell next only mentions (*t*) what he calls "a reason why there must be an arc involved," and in the same ignorance as always of what Hegel is at, remarks, "Probably my readers have had a sufficient specimen of Hegel's mode of dealing with these matters."

He then proceeds to Hegel's "*proof*" of Kepler's third law (*u*). The defect of Whewell's translation in this reference may stand for the defect of his intelligence.

The references under (*v*) and (*g*) concern "*reflexion*," and only illustrate what in that connection has been already said.

The remarks under (*k*) and (*l*) which follow concern "*Perturbations*." They point out that Hegel here admits the law of gravitation, and manifest the consequent perplexity of Dr Whewell, who has always supposed him—*sans phrase*—to deny it.

The last thing Dr Whewell notices is (*x*), that Hegel compares universal gravity to a good thought, and particular gravity to a bad one, and opines that though both are (as gravit*ies* or as thoughts) the same, yet still the difference is. It is quite intelligible how to Hegel universal gravity, as being infinite, should be nameable *good*, while particular gravity as being in the finite sphere, should be nameable *bad;* it is precisely so with thoughts.

Dr Whewell closes with (*w*) Hegel's allusion to "the blessed gods." To the Jovine serenity of Dr Whewell this is too clearly ludicrous, and a thing only to be named. Others, in these days, share Dr Whewell's conviction, and think they have only to point to these "blessed gods" to ensure the instant disappearance of all benighted wretches whatever who would see anything in Hegel. Is this really the case, however? Has Hegel really reason to feel shame of his allusion, or any man after him? The reader can consider the passage (*w*) for himself.

Reader and writer, doubtless, know the law of gravitation to be true, as others do; so did Hegel. That is no reason, however, why Hegel should not develop free motion from the notion, and represent it as it is—as something absolute. There is no man who may not be perfect master of the *Principia* and the *Mécanique Céleste*, and yet who may not, in view of Hegel's conceptions of absolute motion, talk of the stars and planets, "*going along, as the ancients said, like blessed gods.*"

Such talk on the part of Hegel is not of yesterday; it all occurs as early as 1801 in his *Dissertatio pro licentia docendi.* Of this dissertation the first sentences are as follows :—

"Quum præter corpora cœlestia, omnia alia quæ natura gignit, quamvis in suo genere perfecta speciem universi exprimant, in prima naturæ vi, quæ est gravitas, sibi non sufficiant, et vi totius oppressa pereant, corpora autem cœlestia glebæ non adscripta et centrum gravitatis perfectius in se gerentia, Deorum more per levem aera incedant: animali illi, quod systema solis appellamus, non alia est sublimior puriorque rationis expressio, neque quæ philosophica contemplatione dignior sit. Et laus illa, quæ a Cicerone Socrati tribuitur, quod philosophiam de cœlo detraxerit, et in vitam domosque hominum introduxerit, vel parvi habenda, vel ita interpretanda erit, ut philosophiam de vita et domibus hominum bene mereri non posse dicamus, nisi a cœlo descendat, omnemque operam in eo ponendam esse, ut in cœlum evehatur."

As usual in such cases, this Latin is somewhat *laboriose*, but it is not hard to translate. The only difficulty, possibly, arises from the phrase "*animali illi*," which, treated as a dative, would lead to a comparison unsatisfactory through implication of tautological terms, and which, therefore, perhaps, ought to be regarded as a slip of the pen or as a misprint for *animali illo*. But this apart, surely that incession of the celestial bodies like gods through the thin air does not bring with it any suggestion of absurdity. The figure is perfectly in place, and it is here precisely as in the other passage of Hegel which has been so much mocked.

Besides this gloss on the important matter of the "blessed gods," this dissertation will be found to contain almost all those physico-metaphysical peculiarities of doctrine at which the physicists special have taken so much offence. Indeed, it is remarkable that these gentlemen should have neglected a Latin statement which they could read and might understand, and should have preferred a German one, for which they were confessedly incompetent in both respects. In the case of this dissertation they would have enjoyed the peculiar advantage, too, of an opportunity of turning their knives in the wound inflicted on the philosophical demonstrator of a necessary astronomical chasm, by the discovery of the smashed planet that so meanly came forward in the very instant to fill it up. For, of the three designs of the essay, the last is to "demonstrate, by a remarkable example drawn from ancient philosophy, what philosophy can do even in assignment of the mathematical ratios of quantities,"—an example that applies the Platonic Timæus to prove the non-necessity of the very Ceres that, non-existent to the philosophical Hegel, was actually then existent to the astronomical Piazzi! Hegel could speak afterwards of this mishap with perfect good-humour. For my part, however, I confess to sorrow that the *Dissertatio* was ever written. The reasoning in it has a crude Schellingian look, and, not to mention the lamentably weak collation of the apple of Newton with those of Adam and Paris, the blunder about the pendulum is very glaringly put. We see in it his general object, nevertheless, to replace mechanical chance by philosophical necessity, while admission at the same time of the principle of gravitation is unreserved. And at last this is plain, that it was no idle appeal of Hegel's, that namely, to his "interest of twenty-five years long in these objects," and in consequence of such facts, we may reasonably allow ourselves a certain confidence in Hegel, especially when we see in the end that it is not physics he proposes to supersede, but only metaphysics.

In fact, it may now be said at last, that, so far as Kepler and Newton are concerned (and it is here we are to seek the very head and front of Hegel's offending in the eyes of the mathematicians), both Whewell and Hegel tell precisely the same story. Kepler endeavoured to detect "numerical and geometrical relations among the parts of the solar system," Dr Whewell says (*Op. cit.* i. 429-431), and "after extraordinary labour, perseverance, and ingenuity, he was eminently successful in discovering such relations; but the glory and merit of interpreting them according to their physical meaning, was reserved for his greater successor, Newton." And Hegel, *in effect*, claiming no more for Kepler, allows Newton no less; for the interpretation of Kepler's laws, "according to their physical meaning," is precisely the "glory and merit" he attributes to Newton. Only, it belonged to the philosophy of Hegel to see, in the *reflexion* of phenomena into an abstract force, *not* what the philosophy of Whewell could see in it; and it is only Hegel's exclusive attention to the peculiar metaphysic referred to, which misled him occasionally into an appearance of direct injustice towards Newton, at the same time that, *indirectly*, Hegel cannot *hide* his sense of Newton's transcendent greatness. It was only natural, too, that Hegel should have a soft side for Kepler. "Kepler," says Dr Whewell, "always sought his *formal* laws by means of *physical* reasonings." And Kepler says himself:—"The motion of the earth, which Copernicus had proved by *mathematical* reasons, I wanted to prove by *physical*, or, if you prefer it, METAPHYSICAL." In a word, Kepler looked at the world precisely as Hegel did; both sought to see in it a whole, a system, a *one of reason.* To attempt to explain the world by mere outside mechanical arrangement, was not to Hegel the great thing that the conversion of this world into the internality of reason—into the substance of this *me*—was. But Newton represented the former position, Kepler the latter, and Hegel had not an instant's hesitation in preferring the spirit of him whose "highest wish was to find within the God whom he found everywhere without." It does not follow from all that, however, but that Hegel might have thought Newton the greater man; and it must never be forgotten that—without intending it—Hegel was infinitely more unjust to Kant (to whom also he acknowledged his greatest debts) than ever he was to Newton.

The true nature of Hegel's feelings towards Newton, and his reasons for them may be easily inferred from the following extracts:—

"Newton (*Hist. of Phil.* iii. 401), famous for his mathematical discoveries and physical reasonings, indisputably contributed the most to the extension of Locke's philosophy, or of the English manner of philosophising in general, and in particular, of its application to all the physical sciences. 'Physics, take care of metaphysics,'—this was his motto; and so, then, science take care of thought. And he himself, certainly, as well as all the physical sciences, to this very day, have faithfully kept to this, refusing all investigation of their ideas, the thinking of their thoughts. Physics, nevertheless, cannot do anything without thinking; they get their categories, their laws, only from thought, and without thought there is nothing to be done. Newton has especially contributed to the introduction into them of the reflexional forms of forces; he has placed science on the position of reflexion, set up *laws of forces* instead of the laws of the phenomena. . . . This is still so. In the beginning of treatises on physical science we read, for example, of the force of inertia, of accelerating force, molecules, centrifugal and centripetal forces, as of stable entities that are just *found;* what are the last results of reflexion are set up as the first principles. . . . It is certainly Newton's merit, that his form possesses great advantages for the mathematical treatment. It is often envy that is at work when the fame of great men is detracted from; but, on the other hand, it is superstition to regard their fame as something ultimate and final." (*Encyc.* § 270, Zusatz).

Of Kepler, Hegel can still speak with correct knowledge.

"Kepler (*ibid.*) found his laws empirically, through induction, in connection with the observations of Tycho Brahe; for separated details to find the universal law, is the work of genius in this field."

I think, then, in view of Dr Whewell's incompetency whether to translate or understand Hegel, we may simply pronounce his relative criticism, a material for the fire only. At the same time, I would not blame Dr Whewell for this incompetency, and only very mildly, indeed, for his precipitation and *Keckheit* in spite of it. I do not say, either, that Dr Whewell has detected no Hegelian bare bits; but I am certainly inclined to say that what he has found is altogether insignificant in comparison with what he supposed himself to find. He has also proved himself unnecessarily fastidious in reference to the apparent ascription, on the part of Hegel, of the idea of centrifugal force to Newton. It would not be difficult to prove, I think, that that idea was entertained by Newton. I may remark, also, here that Dr Whewell had directly before him certain pleasant proofs of Hegel's honesty which it might have been fair to have signalised. The first of the following quotations is given, in his own way, by Dr Whewell, and the others are in the same neighbourhood.

"If now, in this way, some main features are assigned as to how the leading characteristics of Free Motion cohere with the Notion, this cannot be carried out into and fuller details of rational foundation, and must, therefore, at present, be left to its fate.

". . . The laws of this motion concern two things—the form of the path and the velocity of the movement. The thing to be done is to develop these *from the Notion.* That would give rise to a science of many details; because of the difficulty of execution, this has not yet been fully realised. . . . The exposition of the solar system is not completed in what has been said. . . . To develop these particular features, that is the harder matter, and we have not got that length yet. . . . I have given here the mere elements of the rational (notional) consideration."

I think, too, it will be evident to the reader, that if Hegel very certainly makes no dishonest claim for himself, as little are we dishonest in our claim for him. Various admissions have been already made, and the deliverance about the pendulum, which Dr Whewell seems only to have contemptuously translated, and left so, without a word of remark, may be now referred to.

We have seen that what was said, in this respect, was, that the slow pendulum at the equator, instead of being explained by the greater centrifugal force which is to be supposed to obtain there, might quite as well be ascribed to the increased gravity drawing it (the pendulum) more strongly to the perpendicular line of rest. A spring balance, if there were nothing else—and there is much else—relatively in place, would, if he had thought of it, have convinced Hegel, to his shame, that he had made "a shockingly bad shot" here. This, then, is a gross blunder, and a blunder of the most elementary kind; but what then? Shall Hegel be consigned to everlasting oblivion therefor? Do we treat our other great men for their accidental blunders so?

On the second page of Carlyle's *French Revolution,* it was once read, and, I am led to believe, still is:—"Look to it, D'Aiguillon, sharply as thou didst, from the Mill of St Cast, on Quiberon and the invading English." Chronologically, the St Cast affair took place in 1758; the Quiberon one, again, in 1795. Geographically, when D'Aiguillon, at St Cast, looked to the sea, Quiberon was exactly at his back, away across the country, some hundred miles off. To have done what Mr Carlyle says, then, D'Aiguillon must have literally followed Mr Carlyle's injunction, and looked very "sharply" indeed—through space and through time.

I am sure I read once in a work of Emerson's, too, that *Chaucer had borrowed from Lydgate through Caxton!*

As a third example, Kant, speaking of two astronomers who were in dispute, tells us:—"The one reasoned thus, namely: the moon turns on its axis, because it keeps always the same side to the earth; the other: the moon turns *not* on its axis, just because it keeps always the same side to the earth." Kant adds: "Both reasoned rightly, according to the position each chose from which to observe the moon's motion." Now this, though Kant says it, is quite absurd. The moon either turns on its axis, or it does not. But if a body, revolving round another, keeps always the same side to the latter, the former necessarily turns on its axis. This, however, is the case with the moon, relatively to the earth; therefore the moon turns once on its own axis in accomplishing a terrestrial revolution.*

Here are three blunders, then, each as absurd as the other, and all of them as absurd as Hegel's. Yet the most of us call Carlyle the greatest of literary men in the world now; I, for my part, think Emerson, and surely with a very large consent, morally and intellectually, perhaps the most perfect human being at present alive; and as for Kant, universal mankind proclaims him the greatest of the great since Aristotle. We may let Hegel off about the pendulum, then! Blunders, indeed, are a matter of everyday, and, small or big, no mortal is excepted from them.

It were idle to multiply words, then; Hegel has been simply misunderstood. Not one received physical principle did he deny; his sole object was to replace, not physics by physics, but metaphysics by metaphysics. That he was wrong in preferring Kepler to Newton—and that is not a certainty—is probably beyond a doubt. I, for one, cannot conceive the eager, restless Kepler as a greater man than the deep, quiet, true Newton. But we ought to remember that there have been countrymen of our own who did conceive this, and to reflect that, if Hegel did prefer, to physics and an Englishman, metaphysics and a German, a German of his native Würtemberg, too, this would have been only very natural on his part. Further, Hegel was not wrong in the *substance* of what he said *for Kepler;* and it is only his *manner* that is objectionable as *against Newton.* That manner, moreover, was but a personal peculiarity, a twitch of the lip, a trick of the voice, and it accompanied him even in his references to those he revered. That being borne in mind, indeed, as well as that metaphysic, and *what* metaphysic, was alone his object, his excuse will be well nigh complete. While astronomers of old rejoiced in a process of bowling, and, at convenient seasons, used to give their huge balls a cast of the hand, a kick of the foot, or a shove of the shoulder, Hegel would have the heavenly bodies dance to the Notion. For in his eyes to dance to the Notion is to obey reason. So it was that Kepler's "Laws" pleased him better than Newton's "Force." To Whewell, on the contrary, Force is a higher character than Law; and Newton's transition "from time and space to force and matter, from phenomena to causes," was to him an advance. Kepler's "relations of space,

* If any one doubts this, let him put a penny-piece on this page, and carry his finger twice round the rim of it, once with the top of his nail always turned to the top of the page, and again with the same spot on one side of his finger always applied to the rim of the coin. The ease in the one case, and the pain in the other, will prove irresistible. Or let him take an iron pillar in his hand, and turn round it with his nose against it—if he does so, he will soon find he turns on himself, and will see that the results are not changed, should the pillar be a million miles round and a million miles off, if, while he turns round it, he keeps but his nose to it.

time, and number," however, could be construed into the Notion, whereas Newton's "causal force" was but a category of the understanding. To bring phenomena to "law" was much more "proof" than to reduce them to a mere "reflexion." So Hegel thought, and we, too, ought to see, perhaps, that when we talk of *force*, we have but reflected a phenomenal *many* into the mere *one* of a word. "Descartes said, that he should think it little to show how the world *is* constructed, if he could not also show that it *must* of necessity have been so constructed." This, though censured by Whewell, who cites it, is the true philosophical instinct; and it was, very conspicuously, the guiding principle of Hegel. It is man's business to explain this spectacle, and he will never cease attempting to do so. But to *explain* is to reduce an *is* to a *must*. To know the former, however, is as absolutely indispensable as to accomplish the latter. This Hegel acknowledged, and though his aim is the philosophical *must*, it is our misfortune to be blind to the enormous importance, in his eyes, of an intimate acquaintance with the empirical *is*.

II.

HEGEL AND MR W. R. SMITH,

OR

THE VINDICATION OF THE FORMER IN THE MATHEMATICAL REFERENCE.

MR SMITH'S paper—already, as regards its occasion, etc., sufficiently introduced in the Prefatory Letter—has the following title :—

"Hegel and the Metaphysics of the Fluxional Calculus by W. Robertson Smith, M.A., Assistant to the Professor of Natural Philosophy in the University of Edinburgh. From the Transactions of the Royal Society of Edinburgh, vol. xxv. Edinburgh: Printed for the Society by Neill & Company."

Further notifications are—"Communicated by Professor Tait," and "Read 17th May 1869."

These, indicated, are important interests, then, which support Mr Smith, and I can only lament the compromise he has brought upon them. In Mr Smith's own words, it is his belief, namely, that what he has to refute in Hegel is "an attempt to establish the calculus on a new and very inadequate basis," and there is no such thing in all Hegel! Hegel never made a mathematical suggestion in his life. Mr Smith has simply deluded himself.

The best way to prove this, perhaps, will be just to produce the actual contents of the notes which Mr Smith asserts to contain this "attempt." This I shall do. But it will be well, first, to hear Mr Smith further in expression of his own views.

It is from page 505 of Mr Smith's paper that I quote as above, and it is from that page onwards that, as he says, he "now proceeds to" the consideration of this "attempt to establish the calculus on a new and very inadequate basis." Naturally, then, we shall expect the chief interest to lie in what follows, but still, when we find that, while only some six pages are allowed this, there are fourteen or fifteen that precede, we shall see it to be impossible for us altogether to neglect these.

These, too, bear their own testimony to Mr Smith's belief in this "attempt" at a new calculus on the part of Hegel. It is in this reference that we have the expression (p. 499), "If Hegel, however, shut his eyes to Newton's notion, he has got one of his own;" and Mr Smith does not "intend to attempt to take up anything but the concrete applications of this notion." On page 497, he promises us that "we shall see" "a Hegelian calculus;" and (p. 493), lastly, we have the words:—"To this subject Hegel devotes his second note, professing to point out a purely analytical method, whereby, without any application of the doctrine of limits, everything necessary for practice can be deduced." These words, I must add, too, are followed by the intimation that said new "analytical method" will be demonstrated to "produce results mathematically false," and to be, in brief, "radically unsound." Mr Smith does not let his belief suffer for any want of manifestation, then, and I can only wonder again at the delusion that underlies it; for there is no such thing as "the attempt" described either in the note named, or in any of these notes,—no, not (as has been already declared) in all Hegel! Hegel never dreamed for himself any "analytical method;" Hegel never dreamed for himself an "Hegelian Calculus."

But there must be more than this in these fourteen or fifteen pages, and we may as well see it. I shall just quote, in the first place, however, what on the part of a distinguished mathematician will place us in a better position, perhaps, to do justice to the veritable action of Hegel in this connection. In the appendix to the first edition of Professor James Thomson's Calculus, namely, there will be found certain remarks on the various modes of opening and conducting the different methods of the higher analysis. Of the Infinitesmal Calculus, for example, we learn that it finds the differential of the product by "rejecting" the "last term" as "infinitely small" "compared" with "either" of the others. "It has been justly objected to the method of Fluxions;" we are told again, "that it involves the ideas of motion and time, which are foreign to the nature of the magnitudes that are the subject of investigation in Pure Mathematics." We hear also that "the method of limits, which is due to D'Alembert, is free from some of the objections to which the methods of Newton and Leibnitz are liable, . . . but the principle on which it depends . . . is still, in a considerable degree obscure." Lastly, we have the following:—

"The method of Lagrange, which has been followed, in its general principle, in the present work, is not liable to any of the objections that have been advanced against the others. It does not, like that of Leibnitz, involve the consideration of quantities that are infinitely small, or of quantities that are infinitely smaller than these. It is free from the obscurity attendant on the consideration of the ratio of evanescent quantities, as in the principles of D'Alembert and Maclaurin; and except in its application in mechanical philosophy, it excludes the idea of motion which is involved in the theory of Fluxions."

Now these remarks of Thomson, and the spirit in which they are made, form a complete key to Hegel's remarks, and the spirit of Hegel's remarks, against which Mr Smith directs himself. Thus, the method of Lagrange, as it is preferred by Thomson, so it is preferred by Hegel; and the latter regards quite as the former what concerns "evanescent quantities," "infinitely small quantities," "the ideas of motion and time," etc. Infinitesimal Calculus, Methods of Fluxions, Methods of Limits, all are approached by Hegel as burthened simply by the difficulties that Thomson mentions; and almost, we may say, that the objectionable principle of omission for the reason of "relative smallness" is the former's sole thought. Mr Smith speaks of Hegel (p. 492) as proposing principles of his own on which "he would base the calculus." That is not so. Hegel has no such principles to offer—never dreams of any such. He knows that the principles of the mathematicians are the only true ones; that they are all thoroughly correct; that "limits," "fluxions," "infinitesimals," all work rightly, all work "splendidly," all involve the most important of principles. But he understands withal that every method has its own dissatisfaction with itself, and mainly because of the mode in which it accomplishes, or in which it rationalises, its rejection of the single term, *d x d y*. Really, that is all. Mathematically, Hegel has not the semblance of a proposition to offer. *Only*, he thinks that, *metaphysically*, he sees better than the mathematicians into the abstract principle of the calculus, and into the interest that determines its characteristic movement. It is in that reference alone he has any remarks to make, and solely at call of the mathematicians themselves. He no more thinks of denying the "splendid" work of the calculus—its matter—than Thomson did; and no more than this latter, or any other mathematician, does he think of attributing unsatisfactoriness to its form. He believes himself, as said, to answer only a public call; and it must be allowed that Professor Thomson fairly substantiates this call. Indeed, to my own knowledge, as late as 1839, this most amiable of men, this most excellent of teachers, this most accomplished of mathematicians, propounded in his class precisely the same views in regard to the various "methods" that were published by Hegel in 1812, or twenty-seven years earlier.

We are now prepared, then, before proceeding to our main work, to consider what Mr Smith advances in his first fourteen or fifteen pages. And the opening paragraph in these runs as follows:—

"It is now many years since Dr Whewell drew the attention of the Cambridge Philosophical Society to the courageous, if somewhat Quixotic, attempts of Hegel to cast discredit on Newton's law of gravitation, and on the mathematical demonstration of Kepler's laws given in the 'Principia.' At the time when Whewell wrote, it would probably have been difficult to find in Britain any one ready to maintain the cause of Hegel in this matter, or even to hint that the astounding arguments of the Naturphilosophie flowed from any deeper source than self-complacent ignorance."

Setting out with these misapprehensions which have now, I hope, been thoroughly disposed of, we can readily conjecture what we have to expect from Mr Smith. Accordingly, it is quite in keeping, that he talks in his next paragraph of Dr Stirling not venturing "to say that Hegel's *proof* of Kepler's laws is *right*." "Proof"—"right!" Is recognition of Kepler's laws as in harmony with the Notion a *mathematical* "proof," then? And is that "proof" *technically* "right?" Really, one must sympathise with the self-complacency of Mr Smith in his own mercy: when Dr Stirling "feels sure that it" (said *proof*) "would repay the attention of the mathematicians," "it would not, perhaps, be impossible," Mr Smith intimates, "to rob Dr Stirling of even that sorry consolation!"

We may take the next three paragraphs together and say that, according to them, the "views of Hegel" are to Mr Smith these—The mathematicians have "never been able to put the higher calculus on a basis thoroughly free from confusion or even error;" Newton, specially, has not been "so far master of his own thought as to be able fairly to deduce the practical rules of his method;" Newton has fallen into "real errors;" Newton has determined the fluxion of a product "in a manner analytically unsound!" Dr Stirling, too, "has no hesitation in pronouncing Newton guilty of an obvious mathematical blunder!"

It is difficult to believe that any one could so utterly overlay and squelch the small mouse of truth here, and by such a very mountain of—misapprehension. The mathematicians have "never been able to put the higher calculus on a basis thoroughly free from confusion or even error!" Hegel is precisely as Thomson in that regard, and I fancy even Mr Smith would not misinterpret what I have quoted from the latter into a charge of mathematical confusion and technical error against the mathematicians. In point of fact, Hegel charges these gentlemen with no "error;" and even the word "confusion" can become pertinent only by being translated into logical unsatisfactoriness—precisely the same unsatisfactoriness that is both meant and mentioned by Thomson. Newton not "master of his own thought!" And it is Hegel who shall have said so—Hegel, whose delight in Newton's mastery of thought is utter and express! Then "errors?" Hegel has to allude to one error on the part of Newton, as referred to by Lagrange, which error Mr Smith allows to have been recognised and corrected in the second edition of Newton's own work. Again Hegel has to allude to an astronomer, Schubert, who shall have "admitted that, in the point which is the nerve of the proof, it is not *exactly* so situated as Newton assumes." Mr Smith's manner of stating this is as follows—"admitted that . . . in the point, which is the nerve of the proof, the truth is not as

Newton assumes it." That, one sees, is categorical, and to accomplish this categorical effect, Mr Smith made a break in his quotation and omitted the italicised "not *exactly!*" Yet one might not be very wide of the truth, if one said, that very *italicising* of "exactly" is precisely the "nerve" of the quotation. Why, then, did Mr Smith omit it? Lastly, in regard to the fluxion of the product, Hegel simply put side by side with one arithmetical result another—objecting thus not to the former result itself, which was right, as he knew, and as everybody knew, but to the formal expedient in justification of it. This last sentence contains the amount of "Dr Stirling's" sin also, and the conclusion of the whole must be that Hegel, *alluding* to one admitted error and one admitted "not *exactly*" on the part of Newton, never, as of himself, or from himself, accused this latter of any one "error" whatever. A drawing near the mathematicians in the spirit of Thomson, then, a delighted acknowledgment of Newton's "mastery," an allusion to two remarks on the part of others, each remark situated as we said, and a mere sly *side by side* on his own part,—that, in regard to Hegel, shall be material enough for those enormous misrepresentations of Mr Smith! All, or most, of this matter, however, we shall, directly or indirectly, see again. Meantime, let it be understood that there is not a single statement in it which is not "schief," *wrong*, to caricature. This one example, in fact, is perfectly applicable to the entire procedure of Mr Smith. Throughout, he has done but one thing only—confounded logical unsatisfactoriness with mathematical inaccuracy.

Mr Smith now explains what he is going to do. "I do not profess," he says, "to be able to treat this question from the stand-point of Hegel's own philosophy;" but the above "assertions" (conceived as Hegel's, that is) are such, he maintains, as "can fairly be examined by one who does not profess to have mastered Hegel's system." Now that, as we see, is decisive, and capable of being used in bar of all further discussion. Mr Smith does not know Hegel, and attributes to him "assertions" which he (Hegel) never even dreamed. Mr Smith's relative industry, then, must be simply a speaking into the air. I shall not pretermit further discussion, for all that, if only for the hope of some not unfruitful results in the end.

Mr Smith, then, proceeds to say that he will independently state the case of Newton, and apply the consequences in test of these alleged Hegelian "assertions." "It is possible, however," he adds, "to go further than this;" and then he tells us of the proposed new "Hegelian calculus," and of his ability, as he declares, to demonstrate it to produce "results mathematically false," and to be in general "radically unsound." Mr Smith's whole "plan" consequently is double: there is, *first*, what concerns Newton; and, *second*, the "Hegelian calculus." We see now, then, the business of Mr Smith's first fourteen or fifteen pages, and as regards their general interest, Newton, we shall have an opportunity for a more advantageous discussion later, when we examine, as intimated, Hegel's own matter. Nevertheless, a word or two may not unprofitably be placed now. Mr Smith's account of Newton's general proceedings runs as follows:—

"Newton saw that there were two ways in which quantities might be conceived as generated. The first of these is that which the usual processes of arithmetic have made familiar to everybody, viz., the addition of discrete units. . . . Newton saw, however, that arithmetic in its most perfect form could give full mastery over quantity, only on the supposition that quantity, as it comes before us in the universe, is always produced by the synthesis of ultimate units, or, in other words, of indivisibles. . . . Instead therefore of endeavouring to eke out this view of quantity by arbitrary assumptions, Newton resolved to return to Nature herself, and inquire how quantity is really generated in the objective universe. 'Lineæ,' he writes, 'describuntur ac describendo generantur non per appositiones partium sed per motum continuum punctorum; superficies per motum linearum; solida per motum superficierum; anguli per rotationem laterum.' . . . In a word, Newton's fundamental position is, that the arithmetical conception of quantity is not that with which nature herself presents us, and is not, therefore, universally applicable. On the other hand, every quantity that has objective reality [*i.e.*, is an object of real intuition] is generated by continuous motion. . . . By means of these profound, yet simple considerations, Newton is at once able to revolutionise the whole theory of quantity, and to substitute for the relation of unit, and sum that of velocity and quantity generated, or, in Newton's own language, of fluxion and fluent."

Hegel would have said all this in a single line. Quantity has two moments, discretion and continuity: you may calculate according to either. Consider what contradictory commixture of the dross and slag of the *Vorstellung* with the metal of the *Begriff* that would have spared! The appeal to external nature for example, and the decision that what she presents us with, on the one hand, is "lines" flowing into "planes," "planes" flowing into "solids," "sides rotating into angles;" and what she does *not* present us with, on the other hand, is "the *arithmetical* conception of quantity!" "The *arithmetical* conception of quantity is not that with which nature herself presents us." Had Mr Smith been even superficially acquainted with the Logic of Quantity he would have known that the moment of discretion was, even with reference to Nature, quite as authentic as the moment of continuity. Nay, we may say more than that; if nature, which is only the external picture or representation of the *Begriff*, is to be the standard, then the moment of continuity—at least as above expressed—is even less authentic than the moment of discretion. Who ever *saw* lines flowing into planes, planes into solids, or sides rotating into angles. And yet who has *not* seen sand and salt and sawdust, berries on the bush, apples on the tree, coals in a sack, peas and beans, and small shot, and a pocketful of marbles? It is in continuation of the same pollution of the *Begriff* with the externality of the *Vorstellung* that Mr Smith proceeds. "This conception of time, as the one absolute and independent variable, is undoubtedly one of the most splendid and fruitful in the history of human thought, and well deserves the attention of metaphysicians." If Mr Smith would only see for himself, he would find that metaphysicians, especially of the type of Hegel, have rather a partiality for such a fine metaphysical *reality* as time. Still we may conceive them to say here—Time is certainly an excellent *type* of quantity, but rigour and purity will dispense with it—rigour and purity will confine you to the notion quantity and its own moments, when you would make a *science* of quantity: *so*, you will be even better led. Professor Thomson had reason, then, when he objected to Newton time, and also motion. In fact, such want of due abstraction is the whole objection of Hegel, in a mathematical reference, everywhere. This we see at once in the single look with which he regards the one interest—the omission of $d\,x\,d\,y$. If, he says, you find $d\,x\,d\,y$ useless, and would fain, accordingly, get quit of it, you ought to consider that it must be useless *by the nature of the case*. Show that, then, and get rid of it so; but, for the sake of logic, for the sake of common sense, do not perform *arithmetical* operations where arithmetical operations have no place, and do not say you reject from a sum—a sum that is still, for all that, to be *absolutely* full—an actual *quantity*—and actually *belonging* to that sum—"because it is *so* small." Really, that is what Hegel says; and it is that Mr Smith has converted into all those monstrous charges of error and incapacity against the mathematicians in general and Newton in particular, just as Dr Whewell converted "Reflexion" and the "Notion" into a denial of gravitation and a new "proof" for Kepler's laws! In very truth, there is not one of these things that is not the chimera of a misjudging brain.

It is also in consequence of this imperfect *Huldigung* of abstraction on the part of Mr Smith that (pp. 496, 497) he begins his attack on Hegel with a little bit of *business*. Unable to see the real gist of what is discussed, and believing simply in a *necessarily* unfounded assault on Newton, Mr Smith lumps together a few incoherent expressions from disjunct pages, and summarily pronounces upon them—

"Hegel coolly ignores the whole foundation of the doctrine of fluxions"—[motion and time, namely, as Professor Thomson did]—"Hegel comments in the most edifying manner;" "Hegel triumphantly refers; and so, upheld by the dictum of this forgotten astronomer, Hegel goes on to inveigh against the mere jugglery by which Newton, already knowing Kepler's results, avails himself of the '*mist of the infinitely little*' to bring out apparent mathematical proofs of these results; one does not know whether the singular perversity of this accusation against Newton's *moral character*, or the incredible ignorance of the argument by which it is supported, is most to be wondered at. . . . A Hegelian calculus, as we shall see, would certainly have been of little service to physics."

Such tossing to and fro, with execration, of *disjecta membra*, is as meaningless as such *disjecta* must be; and we cannot wonder that he who finds in Hegel a *new* "analytical calculus," can find in him also "an accusation against Newton's moral character!"

What Hegel means about Kepler's laws and Newton's "proofs," Mr Smith simply fails to understand. Hegel, as we saw already, has been told—*I* don't say by Newton, but certainly by others—that these "proofs" amount to a supersession of the "discovery;" and he simply remarks the "discovery" must stand on its own legs—no mathematical process, purely as such, is adequate to the discovery of any new fact in experience. It is just possible, all the same, that the "incredible ignorance" must change sides. It is in this neighbourhood that a note refers to Dr Stirling as having "read" a *nur* for a *nun;* and there is no doubt but that Mr Smith is correct so far. The *nur* was seen; but, as memoranda remind me, it was deliberately changed, as atopical, into a topical particle of transition *nun*. This, possibly, too, had better remain so, notwithstanding the air of correctness to the contrary due to—Mr Smith's judicious collocation of passages.

This note is appended to the following quotation from the *Secret of Hegel*:—"Newton only explained what he means by his terms, without showing that such a notion has internal truth." Mr Smith rejects this criticism of Hegel's, but seems to allow it some weight, *if* we are "to pay no regard to considerations of velocity and motion." That, however, is to Mr Smith not so: we must pay such regard; we must have recourse to "actual intuition," and, in that respect, "Newton's definitions enjoy fully the advantage which Kant ascribes to mathematical definitions in general." Such definitions Mr Smith intimates, "cannot err, because they simply unfold a construction by means of which the notion is actually produced." Now this to Hegel is simply the reversal of philosophy. To him it is not the "construction" (the *Vorstellung*) produces the "notion" (the *Begriff*); but, on the contrary, the latter the former. So it is that Hegel is not likely to quake before any "intuition," even Kant's. Leaving aside discussion of the *rôle* of intuition at present, let me illustrate something of Hegel's meaning in this connection by a reference to one of Mr Smith's utterances in this place.

"That quantity which, varying according to a definite rule, always represents at any given time the ratio of the increments, may still be constructed when the time is made zero, and is now equal to unity, or is equal to the ratio at which the increments *start*." Now that, said as against Hegel, is what Hegel himself is always saying. It is about the main thing, in fact, that he has to say. *Only*, Mr Smith says it in the language of the *Vorstellung;* Hegel, on the other hand, in the language of the *Begriff*. What is concerned, says Hegel, is a *qualitative* ratio. It is capable of appearing in various empirical quantities, and under various empirical conditions, according to the nature of the empirical case; but to obtain it—it itself—it in its purity

—it as it only *qualitatively* is—all these must be abstracted from. You only muddle and puddle the notion—the *quality*—that that Newton himself declares independent of *quantity*—by all these mixed expressions, *through* which the due abstraction only *shows*, but to an eye that is educated.

One wonders, indeed, to find Mr Smith so obstinately persisting in the sort of mere rough and ready of the *Vorstellung*, at the very moment that he quotes, and with the import of the *Begriff*, as clear writing of Hegel's own as is well conceivable. For example, on the sentence—"The limit of a qualitative relation is that in which it both is and is not, or, more accurately, that in which the quantum has disappeared, and there remains the relation only as qualitative relation of quantity," he can only comment thus :—

"This sentence must mean that in the equation Lt $\frac{\delta y}{\delta x} = \frac{\dot{y}}{\dot{x}}$ the left hand side vanishes as quantum in the same sense in which δx and δy vanish, or, as Hegel often puts it, $\frac{dy}{dx}$ is 'infinite,' just as truly as δy and δx. Now, we are told again and again that the 'infinity' of the δx and δy does not lie in their being infinitely small, but in their having ceased to be any determinate magnitude, and only representing the qualitative principle of a magnitude. To this statement Newton would probably not have objected . . . But certainly he would never have dreamed of admitting that $\frac{\dot{y}}{\dot{x}}$ is also indeterminate ; for both numerator and denominator of this fraction are in their nature definite quantities. That the fraction can be expressed as $\frac{o}{o}$ is to Newton by no means the essential point. On the contrary, he argues distinctly that $\frac{o}{o}$ must have a definite value . . . To Hegel, however, the fascinating element is just this $\frac{o}{o}$, which for his ends would be quite spoiled by being evaluated. That would reduce it to a mere quantum ; but, in the meantime, it is 'a qualitative relation of quantity,' which is a far finer thing. Not unnaturally, however, Hegel has now to ask himself, what is to be the practical use of this Lt $\frac{\delta y}{\delta x}$, which certainly 'expresses a certain value which lies in the function of variable magnitude.' In asking this question, he still supposes himself to be criticising Newton and the mathematicians, and accordingly proceeds, with much severity of manner, to knock down the indeterminate $\frac{dy}{dx}$ which he has just set up."

Now, I can hardly find a single relevant word in all that. It is probably quite as pertinent to Confutsi as it is to Hegel. I have translated or "conveyed" the entire note, and considered it a score of times; but I really do not know in it anything that Mr Smith is talking of. It can only seem to me as if Mr Smith, desperate at being unable to make a continuous reading of Hegel, had just wildly grasped up handfuls here and there, that he might once for all seem to say something. In the sentence Mr Smith quotes, for example, Hegel appears to me to be talking perfectly generally, and to have no symbol whatever before him, whether to vanish left or to vanish right. That much is correct: that what is called infinitely *little* is only qualitative, and is neither little nor great, nor quantitative at all. Still it is utterly incorrect, for all that, to suppose that Hegel denies it a quantitative *rôle*. Something incapable of being "evaluated," that Hegel should desire *that*, it is impossible to conceive anything more absurd. It is not certain, either, though what it *represents* may prove fascinating to him, that the symbol itself $\frac{o}{o}$ has any charms for Hegel. On the contrary, he seems to argue, as in reference to Euler, as well as in this neighbourhood itself, that Zeros are not happy counters in such a service. In fact, I should say that, to Hegel's mind, all these symbols, meaningless in themselves, only represent a certain qualitative relation, and may be regarded as definite so; but quantitatively they are only possibilities and indefinite till applied in some particular problem. I, for my part, do not know any meaning x has in and of itself, and yet I do know it to be extremely useful in algebra. When Mr Smith, then, calls any of these symbols "definite quantities," simply as they appear, I must admit him to differ from Hegel, but then I must avow also that I do not understand him. Nay, I must avow that I cannot believe, though Mr Smith says so, that Newton himself regarded such mere symbols as possessing "definite values." All this seems to me wide only, and still more what follows:—"In asking this question," Mr Smith observes, "Hegel still supposes himself to be criticising Newton and the mathematicians, and accordingly proceeds, with much severity of manner, to knock down the indeterminate $\frac{d\,y}{d\,x}$ which he has just set up." The question Hegel is supposed to ask himself is referred to what in his note, concerns the Method of Limits; but there Hegel has quite ceased to have any thought of Newton; Newton's correspondent place in the general critique is even some dozen pages earlier. Yet Mr Smith holds that Hegel, "in asking this question, still supposes himself to be criticising Newton!" This I may call wide, then; but as for the felling of $\frac{d\,y}{d\,x}$, that I must pronounce fairly *out of sight*. Hegel, "with much severity of manner," shall have knocked down what he had just set up! Though Hegel cannot be said to have set this symbol up, he certainly seems to have accepted it from the mathematicians with complete satisfaction. To hear that he shall have knocked it down, then, fills me with surprise, and I exclaim where? how? why? But we have now entered on Mr Smith's critique in regard to particulars, and I shall defer its further consideration till we draw into sight Hegel's own work.

This work is contained in the three long mathematical notes with which the second chapter of *Quantity*, in the first volume of the *Logic*, terminates. These notes fill nearly one hundred octavo pages, and it is evident that any detailed treatment of them is impossible for us here. Mr Smith confines his attention to the first two of these notes; but I, for my part, shall extend consideration to the whole three of them, and even begin with the last.

The centre of this note is Cavalleri's method of indivisibles: all else that is said in it is either suggested by, or receives meaning from, this method. According to Cavalleri, "all magnitudes," says Thomson, "are regarded as resolvable into *indivisible* elements, or elements so small as not to admit of farther division, . . . thus, a parallelogram is supposed to be made up of straight lines parallel to one of its sides." Now, what Hegel wishes us to see here is that the essential consideration is of *quality*, and not of *quantity*. It is a mistake to lay any weight on the *number*, the *empirical amount*, the *quantity* that may be concerned. In the parallelogram, the idea of Cavalleri being *purely* applied, we are to see the essential consideration to be *quality*. There is present in it a single regula, a single proportion, which is determinative of it. That regula, that proportion is wholly qualitative; it is no actual fixed empirical amount. It is the spiritual soul, as it were, of the actual parallelogram; while to this soul the parallelogram itself is but as representative body. The parallelogram is but *Daseyn*—as it were, so much representative *proexumbration*, *Vorstellung*,—to a certain *Begriff*, which in itself and as such is qualitative,—independent of any assignable quantity whatever. Nor, indeed, is it different with the other "methods;" in these, too, what is essential is qualitative, and the whole confusion arises from the necessary quantitative expression—representative body—being alone, or one-sidedly, regarded. And this may be illustrated thus:—To multiply the numerical expression of one line into the numerical expression of another line is to obtain—externally—only so much more line, only so much more magnitude of the same sort. It is not considered—the numerical expression being alone before us—that a change of *quality* has taken place, that a line multiplied by a line has passed into a square, etc. All the same, the incommensurability—the difference of quality—that is present, will make itself sensible—in the interminable or infinite series. Continua are not discreta, right lines are not curves, the diameter differs in quality from the circle; and the incommensurability that arises when these respective pairs are treated as homogeneous is the sign of the difference. In this, then, we see that what is active and operative in Hegel is still—even in this sphere—the Notion. He would inform mathematics, too, with the *speculative regard*. Under that regard the "infinitely little" is but the qualitative regula or principle in quanta; and in effect, it is actually present to the instinct of mathematicians, so, though confusion of expression arises from still viewing it as infinitely *little*, that is, as quantitative. The expedient to remove the difficulty, the state of the case not being thoroughly seen into, has really been introductive of the difficulty. What alone is concerned is to give adequate quantitative body, when actual concrete cases occur in demand, to a certain qualitative *species* that is always self-identical. The true infinite is the *regula* itself, not its repetition into mass, its *proexumbration* into a body.

But to return to the method of Cavalleri—he distinguishes in a continuum its external existence—its natural magnitude as it is there—and its principle, that relation of elements which prescribes its precise qualitative (geometrical) nature, whatever be its quantitative (arithmetical) size or amount. The principle may be called the determinant, the infinitely little (*i.e.*, non-quantitative) unit, the common figure of relations, the shape, the species, the regula, the proportion, but a qualitative proportion that is neither small nor great, all question of actual quantity being eliminated from it, etc. In fact, it is not any quantitative infinite that we are to see here, but a certain fashion of *limitatedness*.

Cavalleri distinguishes, then, between external existence and the specific or essential constitutive character—between the body and the soul. There is a *Daseyn*, an outward bulk; but the secret of it is an inward invisible form, which withdrawn, the whole bulk vanishes. This is the sort of attendant vision with which we are to see Hegel approach everything. Always he universalises a particular into a singular. That, as said, is the speculative regard; it is the Notion itself; and Hegel attributes it here, more or less, to Cavalleri. There is a single qualitative shape—prototype. We are to see this *intellectually*, and, as it were, *through* the outside *Anschauung*. When we have the *plan*, we need not carry about with us so much stone and lime. The outside *Anschauung* being viewed as the *continuum*, the *regula* may be regarded as the *discretum;* but it were a false conception, that of the *continuum* as *made up* of an infinite number of *discreta* (regulae) infinitely small. Such continuum is but *exemplification, proexumbration, externalisation* of the regula, and is there—(cannot but be there, nature and νοῦς being thought of!)—from the mere proportion, the mere law of the regula; it is not *composed*, made up of regulae at all. (The regula, in fact, is the *true* continuum.) The arithmetical expression, operated upon or with, may be an infinite series; but still the regula is alone the *affirmative* element present, while the infinite of expression is what is *negative:* negative in this way, that it is only the particular to the universal—the *application* of the regula; or in this way, that it is quantity to quality; or in this way, that it expresses the qualitative difference, the inexhaustible incommensurability of kinds. We have but here in fact, as always, what we have on the great scale in reference to the universe. Nature is to mind simply in the same relations. It is but a quantification of quality, a particularisation of the universal (the regula); and the one can be reduced—arithmetically, so to speak—to the other only by the method of infinite series, which only names the existent incommensurability, and never annuls it. Nature's infinite out-and-out, its infinite difference, is but as these infinite series, when compared with the qualitative universal (νοῦς) from which it flows.

What has just been said constitutes (though, of course, there are *additions*) not much less than the main gist of this whole paper (No. 3.) What is ancillary I may mention now.

In case of any mistake, let me say, in the first place, that what refers to $s^3 : t^2$ bears on Hegel's attempt to rationalise (into the Notion) free mechanics, the mechanics of the heavens. He would like that, with this view, the s^3 could be used as the space-factor, the geometrical one, and the t^2 as the time-factor, or arithmetical one.

Perhaps his very best hit here concerns the expedient of superposition in geometry. He shows that certain pieces being given, in which the determinating peculiarity is exhausted, the question is only of a *single* figure (triangle—say), and that the resort to superposition is but a childish help to mere external perception.

What occurs in reference to trapezoid and rectangle, the comparative areas of circle and ellipse, etc., but meets possible objections.

He makes good use of Tacquet's blunder in reference to Barrow and the cone, by showing that the difficulty arose wholly from the *quantitative* consideration, and would not have existed had the *qualitative* one been thought of. Here, too, as regards the "characteristic triangle," the thing is asserted to lie in the relation of the elements, and that it hides this to direct attention only to what is curvilinear being viewed as rectilinear. I may refer now to what Hegel says in this note of his general object as regards the principle of the calculus.

In the beginning of it he states his result to be that the *qualitative* element is the main one as regards the calculus—the affirmative bearing that at once arises on application, and that it is connected with power-forms and the relation of the derived function to the original power. In the end of it he speaks thus:—

"The intention of these remarks has been to signalise the *affirmative* meanings which, in the various applications of the infinitely little, have been, so to speak, left in the back ground, and to wrest them free from the nebulosity in which that category, merely negatively held, has hitherto concealed them."

In Cavalleri's method of indivisibles, for example—we may, paraphrastically, go on thus—the *affirmative* side is the elementary principle as a whole of relations of the magnitudes concerned, independent of the actual how much (quantity) of these magnitudes themselves. They are magnitudes, and so, necessarily, quantities, and quantitative; still as geometrical magnitudes they involve relations; these relations constitute their quality; it is this quality which prescribes the magnitudes, each its own special nature, independent of the actual empirical amounts in which they may be present. The analytic expansion, in general, has the simply arithmetical form of a number of terms arithmetically homogeneous, and without manifestation, in their relations so, of the qualitative reference that is really present and alone the interest. We have nothing before us, in the first instance, but what is of an ordinary quantitative or arithmetical nature, and suggests no other treatment. But the instant there is *application* of the analytic relations—to actual objects, namely,—the qualitative implication appears, in the form, that is, of the transposition of what is linear into what is planar, of what is discrete into what is continuous, etc. In a word, in the *arithmetical* transition, the *geometrical* (or qualitative) one is lost sight of. It has been usual, indeed, only to signalise the negative (quantitative) and not the affirmative (qualitative) element. Or the latter (qualitative) element has still been regarded as quantitative, but in an infinitely small degree, or as an infinitely little. The very fiction of an infinitely little has been resorted to for no other purpose than to meet the qualitative requirement, and it is just this that has been lost sight of in the, so to speak, arithmetical or quantitative treatment. The geometrical continuity of the construction in space, which may be concerned, for example, has been figured as composed, made up of an infinite number of these infinitely littles. Now this never-ending number is a *negative* assignment: it never comes to an affirmative. The infinitely little is itself negative, for it names quantitatively what—unless in mere vehicle, so to speak—is not quantitative at all (the phrase *infinitely little*, all the same, involves in itself *both* characters); and quantity is the negative of quality, the particular to its universal. In general the practice of directing exclusive attention to the infiniteness of the elements is in every way negative; for it conceals the true interest. It is negative also in this way, that there is present an original difference of elements which is the true source of the unending series between the two. Or the infinite, the irreducibleness, the constant non-success depends on the negative that, though latent, is always actually present in this, that what is treated as discrete is really continuous, what as straight really curved, etc. The fiction of the infinitely little cannot extinguish the difference, which is ever, in the end, cast up, like the sandal ot Empedocles. You cannot treat this quality of quantity as that one without introduction of the infinite series, which is the practical rift between the pieces. For difference is always negative—a presence of *two*, a non-coalescence, a not meeting, a disagreement, an over-lapping, etc. And such is the result always where, though quality is present, quantity is alone attended to. The arithmetical expression of a square, taken only arithmetically, is transition to a lower dimension. What, arithmetically, is a simple multiplication, is, geometrically, the production of a plane—a change of quality; and that introduces the inevitable watershed of which the infinite series is only the sign. Insight into the thing itself, then, is all that is required for intelligence of the mathematical infinite, whether as in series or as in the fiction of infinitesimals.

This is the gist of what Hegel says in his Remark 3, and pretty well the gist, at the same time, of all that he has to say in the mathematical reference generally,—not without errors, be it remarked, however, either of press, or pen, or both. I turn now to Remark 1.

Its theme concerns wholly and solely the metaphysical notion that underlies the introduction of the calculus, and the special peculiarities of the various proposals in migitation of the difficulties involved in the usual mathematical explanations and expressions of this notion. That is, there is no matter in it that is not metaphysical, though in mathematical reference, and there is not a single mathematical suggestion. Accordingly, it is attempted to be proved that, while all the proposals to remove the starting difficulties are philosophically defective, the mathematical infinite—what is concerned in the calculus—is a relation, a law, of quantities, not as they are *quantitatively*, but as they are *qualitatively*, in each other's regard. And it is contended that this idea is *implicit* in every usual explanation of the beginning principle, but not, nevertheless, expressed purely or abstractly enough by any of them. With Newton's explanations, however, Hegel's satisfaction and delight cannot be suppressed. He quotes, with positive enjoyment, many phrases here that, in the delicate incisiveness of their metaphysic, wonderfully resemble those peculiarly his own; and his objections to unnecessary concrete accessaries are more gentle in the case of Newton than is usual with Hegel. In short, in this note Hegel's whole business is to *see* the interest concerned in its own *exact specific quality*, and then to name it with *intellectual consistency* and *logical accuracy;* and the result of the whole is this, that the mathematicians are *substantially* right, and let them gain the most they may from Hegel, that *most*, whatever it may be theoretically, would have no essential effect whatever on their work.

We may say, in a word, that the paper has no object—mathematical imperfection of explanation and expression apart—but to show that the principle concerned in the calculus is simply quantity in the simple *notion* that constitutes it; and that notion may be said again to be simply quantity *reflected into its own self.* The phrase may appear without meaning, but it will not be difficult to find it one.

A reference of Hegel's to Newton (*Logik*, i., p. 305), I translate (*Secret of Hegel*, ii., p. 357),—with slight modification now—thus:—

"These, Newton's *generative magnitudes* or *principles*, are not more interesting than the *generated magnitudes*. A *generated* magnitude (genita) is a product or quotient, rectangles, squares, or sides of these,—in general a finite magnitude. Such magnitude being considered as variable, as in continual movement and flux, increasing and decreasing, he understands by the name of moments its momentary increments or decrements. These, however, are not to be taken as particles of a definite magnitude (particulæ finitæ) Such were not themselves moments, but magnitudes generated out of moments; what is to be understood is rather the principles or beginnings of finite magnitudes in process of becoming."

Now this that we have here from Newton is quantity *reflected into itself*,—quantity not in its externality as an actual empirical so much, but quantity in its internality as first principle, as notion.

That is, as we saw suggested already in Mr Smith's metaphysic of these matters, there are two modes of viewing quantity—the mechanical and the dynamical; the one giving rise to the arithmetic of discretion, and the other to the arithmetic of continuity. Now, it is the latter, opposed as concrete to the former as abstract, that is by much the more important. *So*, quantity is as intensive magnitude, as infinite moment, as element; it has collapsed into the simple intensity, into the specificity, of its own quality, of its own distinctive qualitative nature, of its own notion. For what *is* quantity? It is never a dry independent unit and something, no matter what all else may be. It is a boundless relativity; it is the indifferent limit. To have *a* quantity, you must have always quanti*ties*. Draw a line between any two things as quantities—either is as it is, not in itself, but relatively to the other; either depends on and is as infinitely variable as the other. This absolute relativity, this absolutely indifferent limit, this flight ever into the Beyond (the other side) that must ever re-collect itself again, cannot escape intelligence if it be steadily looked at. Quantity, then, has no meaning, so to speak, by itself. If no quantity were but that of a pea, a pear, a solar system, the one were as good as the other. Absolutely, a pea is not small; absolutely, a solar system is not great. It is absurd, then, to lose one's self in the external immeasurableness that a one-sided use of the moments of quantity leads to. It is futile to "pile these millions upon millions up," they all lie in the one notion,—and that is the reflection of quantity into itself. This notion attained, it is self-stultification to go on repeating its moments as in externality. Quantity has no meaning but as in relation,—that is, as reflected into itself from the relation.

Now, this describes what Newton sees in his dynamical quantity—in those principles of becoming, those moments, those non-quantitative beginnings into which he would conceive all actual quantities reduced, and so acquire new power over them. A square is a quantum; but it may be conceived as increasing or decreasing, and if it be so conceived, there can be conceived also to lie in it a principle that, whether there be increase or decrease, is always the same—infinite, then, non-quantitative, qualitative only; and, reflected into *it*, the square is reflected into itself.

But the calculus is simply an application of this notion. In it we have to determine in regard to concrete quantities mutually inter-dependent. These are reflected into themselves, or made non-quantitative, and the relation between them is similarly reflected into itself or made non-quantitative. So we have $\frac{dy}{dx}$. Hegel is quite correct, then, in pointing out that to refer to motion, to increments, etc., is to disturb the abstraction we ourselves have reached.

Ever, however, there are the two sides. There is no such thing as dynamical quantity alone, or mechanical quantity alone. The arithmetic of discretion is the necessary body (the Für-Eines) to the necessary soul (the Für-Sich). And this names the mystery of the world: this names the *notion*. The misfortune is that the world can see only one side of this notion at a time. Most men, indeed, take either *one* side or the *other*, and thus remain hopelessly *abstract*. Nature, the Senses, that is the mechanical side—the side of the arithmetic of discretion; and it can yield no infinite but the spurious one,—the boundless out and out,—the *Progressus ad infinitum*. The true concrete man is he who preserves his humanity, and who insists on the *return* —the return of quantity into itself, of the Für-Eines into the Für-Sich, of the abstract discretes into the continuity in which alone they have meaning.

For the *notion*, and for the notion here concerned, we must always figure an abiding relation—the *return*—the return from an expressing body into an expressed soul. That is the typus of the universe. Hegel calls it "the infinite difference," as it were the infinite disjunction, the infinite *dif-ference* of the two brought into the one—into the one of the single specificity. Two go to the bent bow, but the result is one. This is quality. And let us persist in the absoluteness of the one side, the quantitative side, we lose ourselves only in the spurious progressus, which, synthesise it as we may, is always inexhaustible—has always a Beyond in it that may not be overtaken.

All this is implicit in Newton's conception of genita and their generating principles. The mathematical infinite is the true infinite, the notion of quantity as quantity, and not the spurious one of infinite external progression. To that, repeat it endlessly as you may, no meaning can be found but in relation; and it can be found as well at first as at last. For the quantitative relation, *both* sides must be sublated. In this way the infinite relativity returns into itself, and is held fast so. The externality is, so to speak, the *material* of the single virtue, but, as infinitely variable, or only relative, it is negated. That is, there is question of quanta—externality—as a Für-Eines, but what is vital is only the Für-Sich—the quality to which that is reduced. We have no question longer, then, of any apparently fixed finite empirical quantity—but of the quality, be the apparently fixed finites what they may. It is that qualitativity that is the infinitude. It is the relation that is the thing; the precise quantity, whatever it be, is only a moment taking meaning from the other in relation with it. Consequently, the quantitativity, *as such*, disappears. Spinosa's expression for the state of the case is, "That the nature of the thing itself exceeds every determinateness"—every quantitative determinateness by which stand might be made.

I pass to a description of the general course of Remark 1 itself.

We are emphatically told at once that it is the *theory* of the calculus Hegel alone considers. It is that that is as yet imperfectly justified; but the practice of the calculus, on the other hand, is said to have fully justified itself—and splendidly so. What, in fact, then, is alone considered in this Remark is the starting act of the calculus—on the whole, the arbitrary omission of the terms after the second—and the various attempts which have been made to justify it. What is first signalised is, that the principle in question, though involving quantitative application, is itself non-quantitative. Mathematicians have erred, in the first place, in not steadily seeing and firmly naming this. The reference to Kant that follows would make good only that Kant's infinite is but the spurious progressus. This is accomplished in the usual admirably searching and infinitely significant terms. What presents itself next as regards the notion of the infinite as well as the Für-Eines, etc., may be now passed as already exhausted. To illustrate this notion of the infinite, however, Hegel proceeds to take up the various stages of the mathematical expression of quantity as a moment of relation, and he intimates his own view to be *implicitly* illustrated by all of them.

The first stage is the fraction. Take $\frac{2}{7}$, for example; that may be as well $\frac{4}{14}$, $\frac{6}{21}$, etc. There is here, then, already a certain quantitative indifference, as well as a certain qualitative unity. The numbers themselves, 2, 7, etc., are no longer seen to count *as such;* what alone counts is the relation—or to take it generally, in a mere fraction there is a one qualitative regula, species, soul, etc., and there is also a quantitative externality which is indifferent to a certain extent, but which may be regarded as the sort of natural manifold or plurality of a body. Implicitly, there is a single quality; explicitly, there is infinite quantity, quite indifferent so long as the quality is preserved. Thus, even the fraction is but a type,—like the universe itself,—of the notion. In it, too, the Particular (quantity) is Universalised (or thought) into the Singular (the quality, the single specificity). Self-reflection is What-is *is.* That is the *qualitative antithesis* that is present everywhere; for there can be no quality without antithesis, and that has the single type—reflection of the many (the particular) through the universal into the one (the singular). But, if everything—if every manifestation be necessarily an antithesis, then, for manifestation, it is necessary that there should be in everything *a* negative, or its own negative. Only so is affirmation possible. Now, the element of the particular is the element also that can be called the negative. This will enable us to understand what Hegel proceeds to as regards the ordinary infinite or interminable series, which, he says, have not their negative within them, and so never reach an end. Perhaps it were better to say that, as they are themselves the bare negative and never reach self-reflection, it is so that they are interminable. The *return* is the ultimate secret,—almost we might say the *return* is the *turning-point* of the universe. Otherwise named, it is the negation of the negation. An excellent glimpse is got into it in what Hegel, after examination of such an expression as $\frac{a}{b}$ (as well as series), goes on to adduce in regard to Spinosa, and the true as opposed to the false infinite. It is here he talks of the true (the mathematical) infinite being only *apparently* burthened with inexactitude, while it is the false (or metaphysical) infinite that is *really* so burthened.

Hegel advances now to higher forms, to further mathematical expressions of quantitative relation, but I may state at once the general result here to be nearly this,—While, firstly, non-quantitative, *variability* is, in the second place, erroneously applied as *distinctive* of such higher forms. Thirdly, again, what is distinctive in the variability itself is the presence of power-forms higher than the first. This last reference, we can understand now, from what we saw in the third note, that transition of power, though arithmetically homogeneous and quantitative, is geometrically and existentially heterogeneous and qualitative.

Hegel thus accurately stamps out the metaphysical nature of the principle concerned, and vindicates it from some general objections as in regard to comparison, middle-states, etc.

In his remarks that respect all this matter, Mr Smith is peculiarly unfortunate. He simply finds himself lost, and talks incoherently. Read, for instance, what he says about Hegel's assertion that the principle is non-quantitative: he actually pillories Hegel for denial of the very quantitative application he is engaged affirming,—"Hegel does not seem to have seen that $\frac{o}{o}$ has a real *quantitative* value!" This occurs *passim* in Mr Smith, but it is only an ineptitude. It is not only idle, that is, but inept, with such things before us, to talk of Hegel as denying a quantitative *rôle* to, the necessity of evaluation for, the various symbols. But very far from seeing that, Mr Smith expressly follows (p. 506) the above up by, "And further there was in Hegel a rigid determination *not* to see the real qualitative difference between the continuous quantity of the higher analysis and of actual nature, and the discrete quantity of arithmetical abstraction!" We have seen already that the allusion to nature, always at least *equally* relevant to the arithmetical side, were better suppressed here; but can one well believe one's eyes in the reference otherwise? Hegel, in these notes, shall have manifested "a rigid determination *not* to see the real qualitative difference" which, as between the continuity of the higher analysis and the discretion of arithmetic, is—absolutely—the *only* thing he does see and endeavours to get others to see! Why, we have just learned that said difference is precisely the Notion—the Hegelian Notion—the secret of Hegel! Hegel shall have manifested "a rigid determination not to see" his own Notion! But Mr Smith has, in his own support, a note here:—"Hegel absolutely identifies *analysis* with arithmetical process—'Auf analytische d. i. ganz arithmetische Weise.'" Now, that is quite true, but that analysis is *not* the higher one. The word analytic as used in the above phrase is used merely etymologically. It is convenient to oppose, as occurs more than once in this very paper, to "arithmetical" "analytical," meaning by the latter what concerns the higher calculus. But an arithmetical amount is very certainly an analytical amount—analytical signifying ana-lytical, dis-soluble, decomposable into discretes. Now, when Hegel correlates the two words, it is in that sense only. He tells us, for example (*Logik*, i. 237), "number, because of its principle (the unit), is a something externally put together as such, a purely analytic figure which implies no inner connection," or (239) it is "a Synthesiren that is still wholly of analytic nature, seeing that the connection is entirely factitious, that there is nothing in it, or comes into it, that is not quite externally to hand." That reference to what is of the nature of a sundering aggregate, or possibly sundering aggregate of possible discretes, is what Mr Smith ought to have seen in what he has converted into its own opposite. But, as said, this incoherence, this *Verloren-seyn*, on the part of Mr Smith, is, in reality, but the burthen of every separate sentence. In what follows, for example, when Hegel, in allusion to what is so capital with him—the changed quality in the geometrical object introduced by squaring, etc., says the relation now is not of x to y, but of x to y^2, Mr Smith, "with much severity of manner," must, rising on his virtuous toes, convict this same Hegel of the ignorant denial of x having still a relation to y! Hegel remarks that, in $\frac{2}{7}$, the 2 and 7 are, each by itself, definite quanta, and that no necessary connection is involved between them, that further this fraction is a fixed quantum, a certain quotient. Even alter the numerator, he says, as into 4, 6, 8, and the denominator, as into 14, 21, 28; nevertheless, the ratio or relation remains the same. But all this, he points out, is essentially changed when we have to do with such an expression as $\frac{y^2}{x} = p$, for example: "x and y," he says, "have here the sense of being able to be definite quanta;" but the question before us now is not of the quotient between x and y, but between x and y^2. Not only the sides of the ratio are not certain fixed empirical amounts, but the ratio itself is not that—the very quotient is as quantum completely variable. It is the introduction of the square does this. "The relation of a magnitude to a power is not a quantum, but essentially a qualitative relation." What Mr Smith sees in all this is that Hegel, asserting the ratio in question to be now of x to y^2, has denied *any* ratio longer to exist between x and y! Accordingly, it is with perfect moral pathos that he cries—"It is needless to say that the man who could make 'no constant ratio' identical with 'no ratio.' . . *is hardly fit to construct a new theory of the calculus!*"

He who finds, when Hegel points to the effect of squaring, that all relation is denied for the root, may well find "a new theory of the calculus" in Hegel, and he who finds the latter may well find the former. In fact everything is possible to him who sees Hegel "set up" $\frac{dy}{dx}$, and still more to him who sees Hegel "knock it down."

But returning to our description of the contents of Hegel's first note, we have now the pleasure of hearing this very Hegel tell us "the thought" that underlies the origin of the calculus "cannot be more correctly expressed than it has been expressed by Newton." Only, as Prof. James Thomson disapproved of "the ideas of motion and time, which are foreign to the nature of the magnitudes that are the subject of investigation in pure mathematics," so Hegel would eliminate what concerns "conception of motion and velocity," because the thought expressed so, is not "expressed in the due abstraction, but concretely mixed up with inessential forms." This "due abstraction," as we have seen and see, is sufficiently innocent and well intended; it is common to Hegel with the greatest mathematicians themselves, too; nevertheless, it is here that Mr Smith actually feels himself, perhaps, securest, and he belabours Hegel with such violence because of motion, Lagrange, and the rest, as might make a Thomson start from his grave. "It was Hegel's misfortune to live at a time when, among other fruits of the Aufklärung, Lagrange's formal and superficial method of treating physics was in great repute; and surely it was a cruel fate that the great enemy of the Aufklärung should, through a defective mathematical education, be made a willing captive to a mathematical Aufklärung which has, from its intrinsic weakness, fallen as fast as it rose." Mr Smith might be quoted to a like lesson as regards Newton, motion, time, etc., and had he reflected that Hegel entertained the same ideas in these references that had been expressed by the mathematicians themselves, being without object, indeed, but to offer help in the spirit of these ideas, it is not likely that he (Hegel) would have been accused of an ignorance he had only received from the mathematicians, or that his propositions would have been met by a wrath so blindly, so contradictorily, in error, as to take for a no what was precisely a yes. That is really the character of Mr Smith's criticism; and surely to demand the same abstraction that the mathematicians themselves demanded, was not, on Hegel's part, sufficient provocation to have his work denounced as simply its own reverse. Nay, this due abstraction itself is probably only enhanced correctness. Fluxions may be to Mr Smith a sort of mathematical philosophy of time and motion; but, perhaps, they ought to be regarded, for all that, as the dynamics of Quantity. This seems Hegel's view, and he is certainly supported in it by the greatest mathematical thinkers of all time, and, specially, by Newton; for Newton's references by way of illustration to time and motion cannot hide the pure abstraction of dynamical quantity that lies in their midst. That is seen in what he says of rectangles, squares, etc., constantly increasing or diminishing. To increase or diminish certainly seems to imply time and motion. Nevertheless, said transition ought to be held as independent of both, and as only resulting in the qualitative law or regula, which is the timeless and motionless *principle* of these quanta. That, at least, is Hegel's quest,—this principle; and that, *implicitly*, we shall hold to be also Newton's quest. It was, after all, really only enhanced correctness on Hegel's part, then, to demand this due abstraction, and Thomson, as we saw, demanded the same.

What Hegel says of Carnot in this place, too, surely does justice to Carnot, though duly signalising certain *impurities* in the general conception.

The next reference is to Infinitesimals. These he affirms to be already implied in, but very much behind, Newton's procédés,—so far as purity and consistency of conception are concerned. It is here that what is mainly in Hegel's thought,—the omission of *d x d y*, comes to the surface, and Hegel now proceeds to consider the various expedients in mitigation or justification of this. Euler, for example, in reference to the disappearance of quantitativity, introduces the conception of zero; but (besides other weak points) to *express* the relation as between zeros is objectionable,—in *expression*, and rather darkens down the essential point, which is the relation as between non-quantitative but qualitative sides (though in quantitative matter). The quanta are assuredly zeros (in a certain way), as quanta, but zero to zero is not adapted to express the qualitativity that still remains. Though this is what is implicit in the whole action, it is precisely this that the action itself tends to render inexplicit.

Fermat, Barrow, and others make the process easy by reference to relative insignificancy, but understanding remains unenlightened—despite the magnanimous attempt of Wolf.

We come now to the capital point that concerns Newton's expedient for the omission of the *d x d y* term. This is the *fons et origo* of all these evils, and demands our most serious inquest. But, in the first place, I will say what Hegel does *not* do here. He does *not* wish the *d x d y* term *retained.* He knows that the correct result cannot be obtained unless *with* its omission. This presupposition in regard to *d x d y* accompanies him, as a condition necessarily understood, everywhere indeed; and it is sufficiently singular that Mr Smith should be unaware of any such constantly concomitant ground-understanding. Mr Smith asserts Hegel to accuse Newton of determining the fluxion of a product in a manner "analytically unsound." Now that not only is not so, but, the "ground-understanding" considered, cannot be so. Hegel knows the result to be analytically *sound;* he only objects to an apparent arithmetical stratagem in deduction of it. Mr Smith's mistake is so complete, however, that he actually tells us, p. 503,—"Instead, therefore, of Newton rejecting a quantity on the ground of relative smallness, we find that Hegel has gratuitously introduced such a quantity,"—*d x d y*, namely!

Now, this mistake of Mr Smith is bad enough in itself, but it is worse in its consequences. It misled, namely, two of our most distinguished men of science into illustrations from steamboats and railway carriages that were quite beside the point. Misled, indeed, into proceedings so superfluous, it was no wonder that they talked of "the incapacity of metaphysicians to understand even the most elementary mathematical demonstrations." That fortunately is not so; the best metaphysicians have always been the best mathematicians; and one is almost disposed to augur badly for the future of mathematics and mathematicians, if it is true that they contemplate dissolution of the ancient marriage. But be that as it may, no metaphysician can feel at all aggrieved at the remark in question, seeing that, in this very paper, there has been such striking and abundant demonstration of at least *a* mathematician's incapacity to understand the metaphysician, or even the logic of his own processes.

What Hegél, in the second place, does do is this,—but, first, let me quote from Professor James Thomson. In the Infinitesimal Calculus, this mathematician tells us, the difference of the function increased by the infinitesimal increment, from the original function is found thus, u being assumed as $= x\,y$:— "Here by increasing x by $d\,x$ and y by $d\,y$, denoting by u' what the function then becomes, and subtracting, we obtain $u' - u = x\,d\,y + y\,d\,x + d\,x\,d\,y$." That, then, is the difference required. Of course, Professor Thomson goes on to tell us that $d\,x\,d\,y$ is rejected as "infinitely small compared with," etc. What we have to see, however, is that, under supposition of an arithmetical process, the whole *arithmetically* "correct" result is $x\,d\,y + y\,d\,x + d\,x\,d\,y$. *Analytically*, we know that that is not so; analytically, we know that $d\,x\,d\,y$ must—for "correctness"—be got rid of. Leibnitz proposes to reject $d\,y\,d\,x$ as *relatively insignificant*, intimating by that phrase, that even so, the *arithmetical* process may be regarded as "correct," quite as well as the analytical one. Newton, too, for analytical correctness, has to reject $d\,x\,d\,y$; but he would effect reconciliation of analysis with arithmetic, he would preserve "correctness" to both, by the following stratagem: When the product of x and y, each being lessened by subtraction of a half of its infinite difference, is taken from the product of x and y, each being increased by addition of a half of its infinite difference, there remains $x\,d\,y + y\,d\,x$, and this is the differential of the product $x\,y$. The involuntary answer is obvious: I see what comes out arithmetically by the turn of *your* hand; but what came out also arithmetically by turn of the correct arithmetical hand was different; and it is vain to say your result is a correct arithmetical result arithmetically deduced from the same premises from which the other correct arithmetical result was also arithmetically deduced; for, in that case, $x\,d\,y + y\,d\,x$ would be equal to $x\,d\,y + y\,d\,x + d\,x\,d\,y$, which is absurd. Hegel, then, does not quarrel with the rejection of $d\,x\,d\,y$, but only with the various excuses for it.

The above, to be sure, is not Newton's language, and Mr Smith almost objects as much; but it is a perfectly fair translation of Newton's language into infinitesimal terms. The language may seem indifferent, then, the problem being the same in either? It is easy to fall into such a supposition as this; but I, for my part, must confess to have been misled by the mere change of language, correct though it be; and it is also my sincere belief that Hegel has been similarly misled. I do not believe that he, for his part, would ever have thought it free to him to change Newton's language, and, accordingly, I take it for granted that he must have been directly under guidance of some mathematical authority other than Newton. Had Hegel studied Newton's own language, he would have seen that Newton was not only perfectly correct in the analytical result, but perfectly unassailable also in the formal process thereto. This process, under change of language, cannot but appear arithmetical. In Newton's hands, however, not only the result, but the process is analytical, and the rejection of $dx\,dy$ is conditioned precisely as Hegel wished it to be—by the nature of the case itself. The expedient, in short, of considering one half on this side, and one half on that, of the point to be determined is really unimpeachable, and, in its simplicity and efficiency, does the usual honour to Newton's extraordinary penetration and unrivalled resource.

The change of language, pre-occupied as I was by its legitimacy, prevented me from seeing this for long; otherwise the truth would have been told—without mention, I think, of Hegel's "harpoon;" and now only that I can tell it, and do tell it—now only is that I am *truly* "jubilant!" Acknowledgment of so much misleading, however, is evidently wholly unavailable in excuse of Mr Smith, who has utterly failed to see what Hegel meant, whether arithmetically or analytically.

What follows, again, concerns Newton, but is not much. It has no object but to show the *dangerousness* of considering, not the nature of the case, but the tempting (though illogical) idea of relative smallness, and resorting, consequently, to rejection of what is so characterised. It is to that is to be attributed a certain error of Newton's discussed by Lagrange, and corrected, as Mr Smith reminds us, in Newton's own second edition. Qualitative considerations, on the part of Newton, might or might not have prevented the momentary oversight; still Hegel has, very possibly, perfect reason for asserting that the whole general difficulty in question would disappear, were the operation made to depend not on the quantity, but on the quality concerned. Certain terms shall have validity, only as containing the qualitative character required, and the rest none, simply as non-qualitative, and not merely as quantitatively insignificant. What is to be looked to is not a *sum*, but a *relation*. All this appears pretty full in the *Secret of Hegel*. As Mr Smith says himself, Hegel leans on Lagrange here so far as concerns the mathematical facts; it is Lagrange, therefore, and not Hegel, whom he should abuse in that reference; the latter only insisting on that peculiar qualitative idea of his as in connection with the material he simply receives. It is in this place Mr Smith asks, "Would not these relations be violated, and all mathematics rendered absurd, if the term that is *qualitatively* important *could* be quantitatively negligible?" That is pretty well *Hegel's* single question: ought mathematicians to allow themselves so unmeaning and dangerous an expedient as rejection on account of *quantitative* insignificancy, seeing that, in point of fact, they reject only because of *qualitative* insignificancy?

Paragraphs on Carnot and Lagrange have precisely the same burthen, and I pass at once to Hegel's remarks on the Method of Limits. These are to this effect. Though the true idea is present, he says, the category *limit* just as little *expresses* it as the category *infinitely little:* neither the one nor the other suggests the relation that is the interest at stake. No light comes from the *word* limit, and neither does the *character* limit enter *as such*, and with relief of intelligence, into the treatment. *Limit* here, in fact, is very peculiarly limit: it requires an explanation of its own, and brings its own difficulties. Neither is the mode in which it is mathematically *found*, logically without inconsequences. And Hegel, in regard to this mode, proceeds to point to the contradictory aspects—in mere general, not analytic reference—which the setting $h = o$, and the introduction generally of such a sign as o, or $\frac{o}{o}$, lead to. It is such contradictory aspect to him, for example, that what has become $= \frac{o}{o}$, should still remain a relation; and it seems to him that there is no gain in $\frac{dy}{dx}$ being represented as $= \frac{o}{o}$ for there is not the slightest hint in any such expression of the single thing that is wanted—the peculiar qualitativity. Mr Smith meets this objection—as we have seen already—with the incredibly inapposite words, "Accordingly Hegel proceeds, with much severity of manner, to knock down the indeterminate $\frac{dy}{dx}$ which he has just set up!" To say that $\frac{o}{o}$ gives no clue to the the qualitativity of $\frac{dy}{dx}$ is to knock the latter expression down. The concluding observation of Hegel here is, that when you press for an explanation of the result, p, in the middle of all these contradictory expressions, introduced by the expedient of $h = o$, you can only force the arbitrary assertion: 'Well, then, if you must know, it is just such and such a co-efficient, and so and so derived.' Accordingly Hegel intimates that that is really just what it is, and that it might have been far better said at once. All that is wanted is a certain term; for that term contains the qualitative law that alone functions, and all the rest falls to the ground, not because of this expedient, and that expedient, specially not because of its quantitative insignificance, but because of its qualitative insignificance.

It is, then, simply the expedient of setting $h = o$ that Hegel chiefly objects to in this place. The whole result shall be supposed to depend on making something nothing at last, which something, if it had been similarly regarded as nothing at the beginning, would have stifled all result in the birth! That a quantity be conceived to vanish is certainly a very common device in mathematics, and quite legitimately so—in expressions that bear to be correct, let the quantity conceived to vanish assume what value it may. For Hegel, then, it is certainly to be said here that what is before us cannot be held to carry this character on its face. But be that as it may, once again we see that Hegel has not in view any internal, material, analytical objections, but only external, formal, arithmetical, or rather logical objections; and once again we are called upon to see also how fearfully Mr Smith mistakes all this.

We have had already before us (p. 113) the first half of what Mr Smith says as in reference to Hegel and the method of limits, and need now consider only the remainder.

In this part of Mr Smith's work the first reference is to Taylor's theorem, and the mode in which the limit is determined; and here, according to Mr Smith, Hegel shall be completely *ébahi* to find p turn up in that capacity, and "not, as it should have been, $\frac{o}{o}$!" It is really almost incredible that Mr Smith should have even dreamed himself to see the things he believes himself to see awake here. The good Hegel never either thought or said that the result should be $\frac{o}{o}$, and not p. He has not a single reference to the result as correct or incorrect mathematical outcome—he has not a single reference in an analytic or material direction. He only points to certain formal logical appearances of inconsistency which certain mathematical expedients bring with them. Under the hallucination, however, that Hegel is disputing the analytic results, Mr Smith proceeds thus:—

"This, of course, is sadly inconsistent; for instead of our fine qualitative determination, here is a stubborn quantum turning up. Now, says Hegel, the mathematicians try to get over this by saying that p is not really $= \frac{o}{o}$ but is only a definite value, to which $\frac{o}{o}$ comes as near as you please. Of course, if this is so, it is as evident as any thing can be that the difference between p and $\frac{o}{o}$ is not a quantitative one. But, adds the philosopher, naively enough, that does not help one over $\frac{dy}{dx} = \frac{o}{o}$. Suppose now that we were to say $\frac{dy}{dx}$ really $= p$ (a definite quantity), as, in fact, mathematicians *do* say, then it is obvious that δx couldn't have been $= o$. Or, if, finally, it is conceded that $\frac{\delta y}{\delta x} = o$ (which Hegel seems to think most likely, since δy and δx vanish together), then what can p be? Now, can any one say that the man who devised this argument knew what he was doing?"

That, perhaps, is the most exquisite piece of fooling ever witnessed—Mr Smith gravely representing Hegel as coming to *reason* with the mathematicians *mathematically*, and all so regularly from stage to stage; whereas Hegel has only *logically* in his eye that expedient of $h = o$! The wonder is how or where Mr Smith got these things. Fancy this, for example: "If Hegel allows that there is no quantitative difference between p and $\frac{o}{o}$, why does he assume a qualitative one?" Ah, me! why indeed? "Or, above all, why try to explain Newton's doctrine without ever deigning more than a contemptuous glance at the one central point of the whole?" Well now, Mr Smith might have seen that—this, namely, that Hegel has not a thought of Newton in the locus cited, but only of what is peculiar to the method of limits as the method of limits. "Can any one say that the man who devised this argument knew what he was doing?" Will it be permitted me to point out here that the "man" spoken of—the only man who "devised" the "argument" in question—is Mr Smith himself? And, in that case, will it be uncharitable to agree with him, that "he knew *not* what he was doing?" Mr Smith follows up, however:—"Hegel boasts that half-an-hour would suffice to learn the calculus; certainly he might have employed a good many hours in unlearning his false conceptions of it." I have elsewhere shown that the "half-hour" in allusion is again a "boast" only in Mr Smith's own Hegelian incompetency; and as for his opinion that Hegel "might have employed a good many hours in unlearning," etc., we now know what value to attribute to it. It is *Mr Smith's* "half-hour"—the half-hour he was induced to bestow on his hasty enterprise—that will appear in the end, perhaps, the worst spent half-hour in his whole lifetime.

Hegel proceeds now to the category of approximation, to the conversion of quantities, to the physical senses assigned to analytical terms, etc., but in this matter there seems nothing to occur that calls for special mention on my part. We can now pass also the opposition between "discovery" and "proof" as in reference to Kepler for the one and Newton for the other; nor need we spend a single moment on the mere hint of Hegel's *Göthesque* optical perversity. All that is to be found at full elsewhere. Indeed I may now say that I have allowed myself a certain perfunctoriness all through the consideration of Remark 1, inasmuch as the whole of it is *conveyed* in the *Secret of Hegel*—and not badly on the whole, perhaps, despite the small number of corrections I have already collected for future use. I pass in the last place to Remark 2.

Hegel has already told us that the object of this note is to be the *meaning* of the differential expression, derived from the expansion of the binomial, or how it may. He will show in what concrete need the calculus originated, and what is the sense of its characteristic movement when referred to the facts of nature it is supposed to manipulate. On the whole, the fulcrum of all this seems to lie for Hegel in what we have already seen, when engaged with the method of Cavalleri: the qualitative conversion, namely, that lurks in the arithmetical ascent to powers. Such qualitative conversions occur in regard of the dimensions of space, for example. So motion, as uniform and as uniformly accelerated. Such considerations, then, are essentially qualitative, and it is with considerations essentially qualitative that the differential calculus deals. Now, it is just possible, therefore, that this qualitative conversion in concrete objects may be precisely that which requires to be connected with the evolution of the calculus. The calculus always concerns equations that contain powers higher than the first, and its movement is a lowering of these by development in quest of a certain relation. It is in this reference that Hegel talks of the power as capable of being considered a system of relations within itself—the original magnitude being so considered, and, *consequently*, as essentially a binomial—and that so regarded and expanded, there result functions in determinate relation to the quantity itself. This relation of the derivative to the primitive is the relation sought in regard to concrete applications. It is obvious, consequently, how it explains nothing to say, the differential is just such and such a term, and the others are simply thrown out. We must see that it is the original *immanent* relation, and correspondent to relations in the concrete—a qualitative relation which is called infinite only as independent of any particular quantitative assignment, not but that particular problems will always involve such. In view of these determinations we may neglect what Hegel says about Indeterminates, Series, the inappositeness of various other expressions, etc., and confine ourselves to his illustrations.

Hegel's nearest specification here is, that the operation of reducing to a lower dimension an equation which is at the same time considered with reference to the derivative functions of the variables it contains, yields a result which is veritably no longer an equation but a relation, and this relation is the special object of the differential calculus. He announces that it is the method of Lagrange supports his references, but he would bring all into its due abstraction. So only will the fortuitous look be banished from the calculus, and all the apparent contradictions of its opening be reconciled to general principles otherwise. The calculus cannot have arisen from or of itself; it must be the result of some concrete need. But in it, as is usual elsewhere, the first attempts would be instinctive rather than fully conscious, and practice would precede theory. In a word, says Hegel, it is in the various Tangential methods that we must find the thing itself in its successive steps from the first onwards. Again, he says,—

"Let us take the simplest example from curves determined by an equation containing a power of the second degree. The relation of the co-ordinates is given by the equation at once in a power-form (*power* meaning any power above the first). Consequences of the fundamental determination are the determinations of the other straight lines, tangent, subtangent, normal, etc., which are in connection with the co-ordinates. But the equations between these lines and the co-ordinates are *linear* equations; the wholes, in regard to which these lines are determined as parts, are right-angled triangles formed by *straight* lines. The transition from the original equation, which contains the power-form, to said linear equations involves now the mentioned transition from the original function (which is an equation) to the derived one (which is a *relation*, a relation between certain lines that belong to the curve). The connection between the *relation* of these lines and the *equation* of the curve—it is the finding of that that is in question.

"It is not without interest, as regards the history of the general question, to remark that the first discoverers were confined to a mere empirical statement of what they had found, without being able to give any account of their operation, which remained, for its part, wholly external. It is enough here to refer to Barrow, Newton's teacher. In his Lect. Opt. et Geom., in which he treats problems of the higher geometry on the method of indivisibles—a method distinct, properly, from what is peculiar to the differential calculus, he communicates (Lect. x.) his process in determination of tangents—"because his friends have urged him." One must read in the book itself, all about this communication, in order to realise a competent conception of how the process is delivered merely as an *external* rule,—in the same style as school books give the rule of three or the proof by nines. He draws the lines, afterwards known as the increments in the characteristic triangle of a curve, and gives the direction, in the manner of a mere rule, to reject as superfluous the terms which, *en suite* of the development, come in as powers of said increments or products (etenim isti termini nihilum valebunt); in the same way, the terms constituted by the magnitudes contained in the original equation are to be rejected (— the subsequent subtraction of the original equation from that formed with the increments); and at last for the increments of ordinate and absciss, the ordinate itself and the subtangent are to be substituted. The operation, if we may so, cannot be given in a manner more schoolmaster-like. The said substitution is, in the ordinary differential method, the assumption, made fundamental, of the proportionality of the increments of the ordinate and the absciss to the ordinate and the subtangent. In Barrow, we see this assumption in its naive nakedness. A simple mode of determining the subtangent was found. The methods of Roberval and Fermat have a similar scope. The method of the latter to find the least and greatest values, points to the same basis and the same process. It was a mathematical craze of the time to try to find such methods, properly rules, and make a secret of them—which was not only easy to do, but for the same reason, in a certain respect, unavoidable,—because, namely, the discoverer had discovered only an empirical external rule, no method, that is, or not what had been deduced from established principles. Leibnitz and Newton, both from the time, the latter from his teacher, had to receive such so-called methods. Through generalisation of their form and application, these masters have paved new ways for the sciences. But they had, at the same time, to wrest free the process from the mere manner of external rules, and have both sought to procure for it the necessary legitimation.

"If we more particularly analyse the method, the actual procedure will be seen to be this,—*firstly*, the power-forms (of the variables, of course), contained in the equation, are reduced to their first functions. But so the *value* of the terms of the equation is *altered*. There remains not any longer an equation, but there has arisen a *relation*—between the first function of the one variable and the first function of the other. Instead of $p\,x = y^2$ we have $p : 2\,y$; or, instead of $2\,a\,x - x^2 = y^2$ we have $a - x : y$, which comes afterwards to be designated as the relation $\frac{d\,y}{d\,x}$. The equation is equation of the curve;—this relation that, quite dependent on it, is derived (above by a mere rule) from it, is, on the contrary, in quality, a linear determination, with which certain lines are in proportion $p : 2\,y$, or $a - x : y$—these are themselves relations of straight lines of the curve, the co-ordinates and the parameters. But with all that *nothing is yet known*. The interest is to know, of *other lines* in regard to the curve, *that this relation attaches also to them;* or the interest is to find the equality of two relations. *Secondly*, therefore, the question is to discover what are the lines determined by the nature of the curve which stand in such relation? But this is just what was *already known*,—namely, that such so found relation is the relation of the ordinate to the subtangent. This, ingeniously, the ancients had discovered geometrically; what the moderns have come upon is the empirical process so to prepare the equation of the curve that said first relation is yielded, of which it was *already known* that it is equal to a relation belonging to the line, here the subtangent, whose determination was sought. Partly, now, said preparation of the equation—the differentiation—has been methodically conceived and executed. Partly, again, the imaginary increments of the co-ordinates, and the imaginary characteristic triangle, formed thereby and a similar increment of the tangent, have been invented, in order that the proportionality of the relation, found by depressing (lowering a degree) the equation, to the relation of the ordinate and the subtangent, may be exhibited, not as something only empirically assumed from what was known of old, but as something demonstrated. The knowledge from of old, however, manifests itself generally, and most unmistakeably in the said form of rules, as the only occasion and respective legitimation of the *assumption of the characteristic triangle and said proportionality*."

Lagrange now, Hegel proceeds to tell us, "rejected this simulation, and struck into the scientific path proper." That means that, in the same connection, Lagrange made no assumption, but attempted to reach the same point by a mode of procedure regular and rigorous. We have to thank his method, Hegel continues, for signalisation of the point that is vitally concerned. It separates, and handles apart, the two processes on which the solution of the problem depends,—that is, first, the theoretical consideration in regard to the finding of the *first* function from the given equation; and, second, in regard to the finding of the concrete elements which stand in the relation expressed by said first function. This latter need, he says, is *directly* accomplished; and then he proceeds to describe more particularly how, and always so, that the inherent agreement with Hegel's metaphysical ideas is made manifest. But the great point of Hegelian interest here, so to speak, is this, that Lagrange, even when resorting to the assistance of "the objectionable increment," is held to do so geometrically, and, consequently, *un*objectionably, or so that the consideration mainly concerned is *qualitative* and not *quantitative*. I have not consulted the original either, but I see no reason for assuming Hegel not to have correctly described what he had simply before him. When I say "correctly," I mean *essentially* correctly; for it is not necessary for me to laud the description as well done, or even to assert it free from such errors of press or pen as I have, not unfrequently, found in the last two of the three *Remarks.* I can say, notwithstanding, that it is precisely here that Mr Smith's main delusion in regard to an Hegelian calculus comes to the front. He actually regards a mere description in Lagrange's reference as "simply an excessively clumsy *adaptation* of the method of Lagrange!" Adaptation! Hegel has no mathematical object whatever: he only thinks, and would show, that Lagrange's mathematics agree more or less with his metaphysics. Mr Smith here also, as in what concerned *limits,* has simply misapprehended what it was all about. He has merely fooled himself into a formal wrangling against a mathematical ratiocination that nowhere exists. Quotation would make this even ludicrously apparent, were one not inclined to spare the printer sundry compound mathematical expressions.

Hegel now seeks further illustration of what he has in mind in a reference to Descartes, on which there is no call to enter, whether as respects Mr Smith or the general subject. What Hegel has specially in view is well seen in his eulogium of Descartes, when he pronounces his procedure "the genial *Griff* of an *ächt* analytical head, in comparison with which "the quite assertorically assumed proportionality of the subtangent and the ordinate with the suppositious so-called infinitely-small increments of the absciss and the ordinate stands quite in the back-ground."

Remarks follow in the general spirit of what we have already seen—that mathematicians fail to signalise the precise thing concerned, and resort, in consequence, to objectionable expedients. That numerical operation may be qualitative transition, is again alluded to. "The equation $\frac{dy}{dx} = P$," it is said, "expresses nothing more than that P is a *relation*, and there is otherwise no real sense to be ascribed to $\frac{dy}{dx}$. Of this relation $= P$, however, it is still undecided what other relation it is equal to; such equality, the *proportionality,* only first of all gives it a value and a signification." Altogether what occurs here seems consistent and to the point. But for the length to which this paper already extends, I would translate it, every word.

What follows next, on Hegel's part, is a certain reference to mechanics, of which Mr Smith makes game thus:—"That t and s in Kepler's law are not variables, but constants determined for each planet; that the equation has no analogy whatsoever with the equation of motion; that its differentiation would be meaningless unless space were filled with planets; and that then it would have nothing to do with 'the determinations of that absolute motion,' are considerations that never entered Hegel's head." What Hegel says is this (and what part Lagrange has in it must be determined by others—Hegel certainly begins by quoting Lagrange):—"The law of falling bodies, says Lagrange, is expressed in the equation $s = a t^2$; the simplest next motion after that one would have the equation $s = c t^3$; no such motion is seen in nature; but then there is a motion expressed in Kepler's law, $s^3 = a t^2$; what the first derivative function, $\frac{2 a t}{3 s^2}$, etc., may mean there, etc., ... must appear an interesting problem, in which analysis would show itself in its most appropriate splendour." So far as Mr Smith is right in this reference, by all means let there be assumed another blunder for Hegel.

Mr Smith's comments on *Remark* 2 cease here, I think, and I shall pass to a conclusion on its remaining contents.

The following sentence in the neighbourhood immediately before us, is very significant as to Hegel's general purpose:—

"The preceding has had for object to make prominent and precise the simple specific *procédé* of the differential calculus, and to demonstrate its presence in a few of the usual elementary examples. Said *procédé* has been found to consist in this, that from an equation of power-functions, the co-efficient of the term of development, the so-called first function, is obtained, and the *relation*, which this function represents, is demonstrated in moments of the concrete object; by means of which so-got correspondence between the two relations these moments are themselves determined."

The phrases do not run well, perhaps, but the meaning will be clear.

One more quotation, and the last:—

"Because, in a certain process of Archimedes, as well as, later, in Kepler's treatment of stereometric objects, the conception of the infinitely little presents itself, this has been often used as an authority for the employment which is made of such conception in the differential calculus—without what was distinctive and peculiar in it having been duly signalised. The infinitely little signifies, in strictness, the negation of quantum as quantum, that is, of a so-called *finite* expression, of the completed determinateness which quantum as quantum is. In like manner, in the celebrated methods of Valerius, Cavalleri, and others, which are founded on the consideration of the *relations* of geometrical objects, the ground-character is, that the quantum as quantum of the object of investigation, which is properly examined only in its constituent relation, is to be put out of view, or rather taken as a *non-quantum*. Partly, however, so, the *affirmative* which lurks behind the merely negative consideration, has not been recognised and signalised—the affirmative which was exhibited above, abstractly, as the *qualitative* determinateness of magnitude, and as more precisely lying in the power-relation. Partly, at the same time, this relation including in itself a number of more particular relations, as that of a power and its function of development, these latter more particular relations have been again supposed to be grounded on the general and negative character of the same infinitely little, and derived from it. In the exposition of Lagrange just seen, the precise affirmative that lies in Archimedes' treatment of the problem comes to light, and accordingly there is given to the operation, burthened with the unlimited progressus, its own due limit. The magnitude of the modern invention *per se*, and its ability to solve problems previously intractable, as well as to treat the previously soluble in a simple manner, is solely to be placed in the discovery of the relation of the original to the so-called derived functions, and of the parts which in the case of a mathematical whole stand in such relation. The statements made may suffice to manifest the peculiarity of the relation of magnitudes which is the object of the special calculus in question. These statements it was fortunately possible to confine to simple problems and their modes of resolution; it would have neither been expedient as regards the determination of the notion, which determination is here alone concerned, nor would it have lain in *the author's power* to have reviewed the entire compass of the so-called application of the calculus, and,—through reference of all the respective problems and their resolutions to the principle which has been here demonstrated,—to have completely carried out the induction of this principle being its (the calculus') foundation."

With these words before us, it is impossible to deny either Hegel's conceptions of his own problem, or the pretensions with which he approached it. The former are, after all, not less simple than the latter are modest. Hegel, in fact, has nothing new,—nothing whatever to propose *mathematically;* he would only demonstrate his own *metaphysics* in the existent actual (*i.e.*, of the calculus), without a dream of subverting it, —without a dream even of correcting it, unless in the interest of mere *logical* simplicity and consistency.

With what radical misconception, and in what lamentable spirit of gratuitous abuse, Mr Smith has treated all this, we have already seen, and I shall now quote from his paper, a few final passages:—

"Since we are told that in the equation, $s = ct$ there is no scope for differentiation, $\frac{s}{t}$ not being qualitative [Hegel, of course, does not say that], we may at least conclude that Hegel does not regard uniform motion as continuous. . . . I do not, therefore, think it needful to go into details on this part of Hegel's method. . . . His method has the same fundamental fallacy as that of Lagrange. . . . An obvious analytical absurdity. . . . I shall, in passing from the subject of geometry, merely enunciate a simple deduction from Hegel's result in an intelligible form. 'At any point of a curve there are an infinite number of tangents, which may be got by uniting that point with any other point on the curve whose abscissa is not different by a quantity greater than unity.' I present this proposition, which is *entirely* due to Hegel, and in the development of which my share has been 'purely mechanical,' for the admiration of all Hegelians whatsoever. . . . These notes show [*i.e.* on Hegel's part] quite clearly,—*first,* substantial ignorance of the subject in hand, bolstered up by some hasty glances at the 'literature of the subject;'" *secondly,* great disingenuousness in criticising Newton, without having ever given his views a careful study; *thirdly,* almost incredible confusion of mind, in so far as he seems to have thought that he knew his own meaning when he really had no meaning at all; and *lastly,* to add nothing more, such a degree of self-complacent arrogance as led him to fancy the results of his 'half hour' more valuable than the fruit of the whole life of men like Newton."

The reader will have perceived that, in describing the contents of Hegel's *Remarks,* I have inserted from time to time the counter observations of Mr Smith. In this way, indeed, I suppose myself now to have done pretty well all that is necessary. That Hegel neither proposed, nor dreamed of proposing any analytical method of his own must by this time be as obvious to the reader as Mr Smith's amusing resolution to wrangle such actual proposition of a new method mathematically out with him. Mr Smith's mistake must prove altogether surprising, indeed, in presence of Hegel's own express declaration of insufficient mathematical proficiency even to carry out the illustration of his metaphysical explanations in the entire compass of the mathematical details. Still, for all that, it is not exactly mathematical ignorance that we shall feel impelled to remark in Hegel,—on the contrary, we shall probably see good reason for entertaining even mathematical gratitude towards him, and just because of those "explanations" of his in a mathematical reference. The mistake of the mathematicians (of the Royal Society) in this connection has been, indeed, utter; to them Hegel, whose every word assumed that $d\,x\,d\,y$ was of course to be thrown out, and of course correctly,—to them this same Hegel shall have held Newton guilty of "analytical unsoundness," *because* he threw it out! How much they have mistaken, too, the spirit of his apparent criticism! I shall have shown, in allusion to the fourth proposition of the first book of the elements of Euclid, that, certain pieces being given, the question is only of a *single* figure, and that superposition consequently is no more than a superfluity in illustration—I shall have shown this, and because I shall have shown this, I shall be supposed to have accused Euclid of incompetency, and to have impeached the principles of geometry in general! Or, to Mr Smith specially, Hegel, when demonstrating the presence of his own notion in the mathematical proceedings of Lagrange, and others, shall be only fighting mathematically for his own hand, like the Gow Chrom, and actually proposing a rival calculus! To Mr Smith—at that time not much more than a youthful student—Hegel, certainly at least *one* of the *two* greatest metaphysicians since Aristotle, shall have shown "quite clearly" "almost incredible confusion of mind, in so far as he seems to have thought that he knew his own meaning when he really had no meaning at all!"

One finds ample revenge for Hegel, however, when one thinks of all the rabid nonsense, not only in English, but even in French, that our mathematicians have written against him,—above all, when one thinks of the twenty-one pages, from p. 491 to p. 511, in the twenty-fifth volume of the *Transactions of the Royal Society of Edinburgh.*

Finally, it may be suggested that it will be only fair to try Hegel's "explanations" by reference to what precedes, and not to what succeeds, the year 1812.

Made in the USA
Monee, IL
04 November 2026

67384989R00085